BECOMING KINGS

The Modern Man's Path to Being Powerful, Purpose-Driven, and Fulfilled in a World That Has Taught You Not to Be

JOHNNY KING

Copyright © Johnny King 2021
All Rights Reserved
ISBN: 979-8-5989-4204-8

DISCLAIMER: The information provided in this book is designed to provide information and motivation and is not meant to be used, nor should be used, to diagnose or treat any medical condition. The author and publisher are not responsible for any specific health needs that may require medical supervision and are not liable for any damages or negative consequences from any action to any person reading or following the information in this book. Or in other words, this book is meant to give you a framework and method for introspection and self-discovery and you are responsible for whatever it is that you discover and what actions you take afterwards. Readers should be aware that the websites listed in this book may change.

I dedicate this book to all men who feel the calling upon their hearts. The calling to becoming a fuller version of who they are today so they can be extraordinary examples of what's possible to future generations of men. Let's pave the way!

I also dedicate this book to my mother and father, Sally and Herb King. It is because of my love for you both that I continue to travel this path in becoming a king.

I love you. I'm sorry. Please forgive me. Thank you.

CONTENTS

FOREWORD 5
INTRODUCTION: The Death of a King 8
CHAPTER 1: The Addiction 20
    Updating Your Operating System 25
CHAPTER 2: The Ordinary Man & His Wound 28
    The Wound and Masculinity 29
    The Ordinary World 31
    The Call to Adventure 34
CHAPTER 3: The Power of Emotional Fitness 41
    Emotional State Management 41
    Forgiveness and Freedom 49
    The Three Levers of Emotions 52
    Emotional Fitness Exercise 53
    The Hero and the Humbled 58
CHAPTER 4: Fears & Limiting Beliefs 63
    The Messages within the Mess 63
    Refusal of the Call 70
    Questions You Ask Yourself 71
    Our Greatest Fears 73
    Strategy. Story. State 76
    Changing Your Story 80

CHAPTER 5: The Target 82
    Dial #1: Your 6 Human Needs 83
    Rewind the Clock 90
    Masculine vs. Feminine 91
CHAPTER 6: Achievement & Fulfillment 95
    Dial #2: An Extraordinary Life on Your Terms 95
CHAPTER 7: The Fork 99
    Dial #3: Decisions 99
    Crossing the Threshold 105
    Man's Natural Needs 109
CHAPTER 8: Your Blueprint for Life 111
    Life Tests 116
CHAPTER 9: The Calling 125
    The 3 Kingdoms of Mastery 125
CHAPTER 10: Your Inner Kingdom 131
CHAPTER 11: bEvening & Morning Routines for Men 140
    Creating a Fulfilling Evening Routine 140
    Creating a Powerful Morning Routine 143
CHAPTER 12: Your Outer Kingdom 146
CHAPTER 13: Your Eternal Kingdom 151
CHAPTER 14: The Code of Kings 157
    Who Are You Committed to Being? 157
CHAPTER 15: Playing Life Above or Below the Line 168
CHAPTER 16: Being a Man of your Word 172
    Reclaiming Your Time 176
CHAPTER 17: Building a Kingdom Culture 178

CHAPTER 18: The Game 183
    What is Success? 186
    Harvard Study Exercise 188
CHAPTER 19: The Foundation 192
    Creating a Life Plan 192
    The Power of Mentorship 195
    Change your Limiting Beliefs 196
CHAPTER 20: The Audit 199
    Keeping Score 199
CHAPTER 21: Rituals and Results 206
CHAPTER 22: Defining Outcomes vs. Goals 218
    Avoiding Self-Sabotage 220
    Values 221
LAST STEPS: Taking a Detox 223
    Standing Guard 223
    Take a Life Detox 225
    Healthy Boundaries 226
    Progress Scorecard 228
WORK WITH JOHNNY 231
THANKS 232
ABOUT THE AUTHOR 233

JOHNNY KING

FOREWORD

SINCE 2004, I have been a coach. The majority (about seventy-five percent) of my clients have been women who seek me out to support them in overcoming challenges and making their deepest desires a reality. They yearn for self-love and acceptance, a career that matters to them, and ways to step fully into their self-expression and power.

And... overwhelmingly, women are also looking for a deep connection to a man—either the one they are currently with or the one they hope to meet. A man who is willing to be vulnerable. A man who is committed to looking within and uncovering issues from his past that need to be healed. A man who prioritizes his relationships and integrity as much as the pursuit of his purpose. A man who isn't consumed by material things but is consumed by a deep desire to love. A man who breaks free from societal conditioning about what it means to be a man and, instead, carves his own path with virtue, integrity, and honor. A man who takes responsibility for his life, leads with both his heart and his head, and still knows how to play.

For many women, this man is elusive, and they truly believe he does not exist. Being surrounded by healthy, whole men has come difficult for many of us. Most of our fathers were raised in a time when the conditioning of what men "should be" meant going to work, not being very present with the kids, stuffing down emotions, and living a very neck-up life. Any kind of therapy or self-reflection was reserved for crazy people and hippies. Then, when we grew up, we often found ourselves disrespected, disregarded, ignored, betrayed, hurt, or harassed by men.

Let me be clear: this is not because men are bad. It is because men have not really had stable, healthy models of what it means to be a stable, healthy man. During the recent rise of the feminine, men have been left questioning where they stand, how they should act, and who they should be.

Just as women are asking, "Where are all the good men?" men are asking, "What does it take to be a good man?"

And just as it is our responsibility as women to do our inner work so we can show up as Queens, it is your responsibility to become a king.

What is a King?

A man who leads with confidence, not arrogance. Who keeps his word. He listens and makes others feel safe and seen. He is willing to speak openly about his past, his transgressions, and his pain without anyone having to pry it out of him. He shares what he has learned and how he has changed. He is committed to his purpose but not so much that it consumes him. He owns his stuff and is consistently willing to grow in his relationships. He is an incredible friend and treats strangers with kindness. He is devoted to protecting those he loves and being of service in whatever ways he can. He challenges himself physically and mentally. He has some kind of spiritual practice that reminds him of who he truly is.

That is a King. And more and more men are breaking down the old masculine paradigms and doing the work to become healthy, trustworthy, loving, reliable, passionate, present, and courageous men. I see it in my clients, my friends, men I work with, and in the author of this book.

Men want to be Kings. And not in the "accumulate wealth, women and power" kind of way. They are seeking a way to retain the masculine qualities of strength, direction, clarity, and action while moving away from oppression, repression, and aggression. In order for men to move into this King energy, they need a guide. A way out of the old ways of being a man and a path toward becoming a King. This book is that guide.

Through his own personal stories and experience, Johnny shows the way through the conditioning that is keeping men stuck in outdated and unhealthy behaviors. He sheds light on the fears men have that aren't often talked about or even known. You will learn how to take responsibility for your life and show up in a way that commands respect. Your values will become your key driving force, you will no longer be chasing success to compensate for any insecurities.

One of the essential parts to becoming a King is knowing how to deal with your inner kingdom—the thoughts and feelings that keep you up at night, distract you, nag at you, and get in your way. Johnny will teach you how to deal with your emotions and shift your beliefs so your inner kingdom is a place of deep contentment. He has had the courage to traverse a lot of roads less traveled, so you can trust him to show you the way.

It won't be easy. You will be asked to lift the rug you've swept things under. You will be required to be 100% honest with yourself and do some deep reflection. You will be called forward into actions that stretch you. And... it will be worth it, because, by the end of this book, you will know what a king is and how to be one.

I want to thank you for picking up this book and committing to completing it. You are not only changing your own life, you are making this world a safer, more loving place for women and children. You will be an example to other men of all ages of what healthy masculinity looks like.

You are becoming a King.

Christine Hassler, master coach, keynote speaker, podcast host, and bestselling author of *Expectation Hangover*

INTRODUCTION

The Death of a King

> "Death is not the greatest loss in life. The greatest loss is what dies inside us while we live."
>
> —Norman Cousins

I WAS STARTING TO GO into shock. Everything in my peripheral vision was going dark, and I felt dizzy—like I was about to pass out. My mind couldn't comprehend what I had just witnessed.

My heart was pounding wildly as I stood, vulnerable, on that craggy, exposed ledge at the far end of "the narrows." We were at an elevation of nearly 14,000 feet, with no cell phone reception, seven hours from the nearest ranger station. And my buddy, Scott, had just fallen nearly 200 feet below where I was standing.

I did everything I could to not lose my shit.

"*SCOTT!*" I yelled down to him.

This could not be happening. This must be a dream. No, no, no, *NO!* My mind was racing.

It was nearly 10 a.m. on the brisk morning of October 1, 2016. Scott and I had been on our way to summit Longs Peak, a 14,259-foot mountain located in the northern Front Range of the Rocky Mountain National Park Wilderness in Colorado.

This wasn't our first trek together, as we had climbed several mountains over the years, and became close friends through experiencing many shared interests.

I remember the first time we met.

We were both health coaches in a predominantly female organization. We had arrived around the same time in Tucson, Arizona for a big work convention. Since Scott and I both lived in Colorado, we were matched up as roommates to share a hotel room. Little did we know, at the time, how much we had in common.

He had arrived before me. So, when I walked into our hotel room, the first thing I noticed was the large textbook, calculator, and pencil on the desk near the window.

Wait, did I walk into the wrong room? I thought to myself. It looked like teenager's things, similar to the graphing calculator I'd used back in high school.

Then I looked more closely and noticed the textbook was all about aerospace engineering.

Oh, wow. Smart dude. I like him already, I remember thinking to myself.

I was unpacking my suitcase when he entered the hotel room. We immediately hit it off. He was one of the most genuine, positive, and intelligent men I had ever met.

Prior to our meeting as health coaches, Scott had been a very well-respected family physician. We quickly learned about our mutual fascination with space, stars, and uncharted galaxies far, far away.

Within a few short days (and over the subsequent years), we became much closer, always choosing to be roommates whenever we had an out-of-state function to attend.

He lived an hour from me, so we'd often see each other at local events, too. And as our friendship grew, we began hiking 14ers together (that's how Colorado locals refer to the fifty-eight mountain peaks in the state that exceed 14,000 feet in height).

Over our time together, traveling, doing events, and being out in the wilderness, I became increasingly fond of Scott for his curiosity and desire to learn.

As we set out on our trek from the parking lot at 3:30 a.m. that fateful morning of October 1, we immediately began discussing the stars and the Milky Way, which exploded above us in the night sky.

His ability to be approachable and relatable, despite the fact he was extremely intelligent, was one of the main things I admired about him. Even though he was brilliant, he didn't have an ego about it. He treated me as a fellow human being on equal standing.

Over the years, he'd become a father figure to me; an example of what I aspired to be, as I envisioned myself at his age.

Whenever we'd travel together, without fail, he would call his wife every evening to say good night. They had a love for each other that was so sincere, genuine, and tender. I admired that, too.

Everything about this man was solid.

He had made his early career out of delivering babies, and now he was studying to shoot rockets toward the stars.

On the outside, he was humble and somewhat unassuming. However, the more I got to know the man, the more I was impressed with the warrior he had within. I could tell, for as gentle as he could be in one moment, if challenged, he could easily stand his ground when needed.

He was precise, extremely intelligent, caring, deeply in love with his wife, successful as a doctor, in great shape, loved his kids dearly, was excited about life, was committed to constantly learning, and was a beast on the hiking trail.

And as if that wasn't enough, he hadn't hiked a single 14,000+ foot peak in Colorado prior to his fiftieth birthday. In the ensuing eleven years, he hiked nearly 100!

The man was ripped and in great shape for a sixty-one-year-old. And that was Scott in a nutshell.

In short, the man was a king.

He had achieved a level in life where he was experiencing abundance in all areas, and he had nothing to prove to anyone other than himself. He had a hunger for learning, because that's what he was all about: expanding his own mind while being of service to others.

He was driven because he loved the journey of continually becoming his best self. The only person he was ever in competition with was the version of himself he was yesterday.

And there I stood, on an extremely exposed side of Longs Peak, screaming his name down 200 feet to where he lay.

As I lived my worst nightmare, a young man's voice cut through my panic, asking, "Hey, you okay? What happened? Weren't you hiking with someone?"

Making his way down to me from above was a man I now consider one of two angels who saved me, for how he supported me that day. His name was Riley.

"I was climbing up this crack in the wall when I heard my buddy slip behind me," I replied. "And when I looked over my shoulder, I saw him sliding down the rock face until he disappeared over the edge!"

"Is he okay?" he asked me. "Can you see him?"

"Yes, I can see him. I just haven't seen him move!"

I began to replay everything I had just witnessed. At this point, I was freaking the fuck out inside. I was doing everything I could to remain calm while simultaneously not succumbing to shock and blacking out.

"Do you have cell service?" Riley asked, breaking me from my mental fog.

I quickly pulled out my phone and looked. "No, not a single bar."

Looking at his phone, he exclaimed, "I do! I'll call 911."

Now, you have to keep in mind, up to this point, everything had unfolded in literally less than ninety seconds. And as I was sitting there, staring down the mountain at my buddy, Scott, with Riley calling 911, I noticed something else happening.

My brain was searching for meaning. Questions screamed through my mind...

What happened? Did he slip on ice, did he trip, did he attempt to take a different route up than I did? Could I have done something to help him? Was this my fault?

It was all of maybe three minutes since the accident, but it was that last question that caused me to snap out of it.

I caught myself in that moment.

Over the previous seven years, I had spent countless hours investing in personal growth work, integrating, and creating greater emotional fitness. I intuitively knew that to place blame on myself for something clearly out of my control was something that could end up negatively changing the trajectory of my life.

It was a more formative moment than I could have possibly known, at the time.

Over the course of the next six months, I spent a lot of time digging into why I would ask such a question at a time like that. *Was this my fault?*

Reason being, I had learned over the two years leading up to Scott's accident that there were three decisions that helped me process what I had witnessed that morning, without my having had to think about them.

1. The first decision—one I now realize I made in nanoseconds that day—was to determine *what I was going to focus on*. I knew all too well even then that what I focus on is what I feel. If I had chosen to focus on how mind-blowingly tragic this moment of Scott's accident was for me, I very well could have gone further into shock and passed out, putting myself even more in harm's way.

2. The second decision I made at that moment was to *determine what something meant*. And in this case, what this *accident* meant. Right then, I was focusing on what had just happened. And my brain's search for meaning brought me to the question of whether I would be a victim or a victor of the tragedy.

3. The third decision I made that morning *was what I was going to do*. Since emotion determines action, I *could* have completely broken down and been absolutely no help to Riley, who was asking me for information about Scott, so he could relay that information to the Mountain Rescue Team.

These questions helped me avoid becoming a victim that day. Truthfully, that level of pain is enough for any man or woman to lose themselves—to succumb to despair, depression, or even self-harm or substance abuse in hopes of numbing away the guilt and shame.

My second angel that morning, Lisa, was a trained mountain rescuer who was also climbing Longs to summit that morning. She came across me and Scott several minutes after the accident. Having also lost loved ones in climbing accidents, Lisa was a huge support as she coached me through what I was going to experience once I made my way off the mountain.

However the more time we spent up there, the more she encouraged me to start the trek back down while reassuring me, considering how experienced she was in high alpine climbing, she would make her way down to him if she could.

I had to come to grips with the fact that, when an accident like this happens, there may never be concrete answers.

Since I was above Scott and with my back to him, I'll never know what occurred just prior to hearing him slip.

So? What was I going to do with everything I had experienced that day on the mountain?

I think leaving Scott that morning was one of the hardest things I have ever done. For an hour and a half, I stood on that ledge, screaming down to him, praying to see him move or show any signs of life. Shock would overwhelm me in waves as I struggled to grasp the reality of the moment.

However, as threatening weather began to roll in (and knowing I was still roughly eight hours from getting back to any form of civilization), and with confirmation from the Rocky Mountain Helicopter Rescue Team that they were on their way, I had to say goodbye to my friend. Now, I've never been in the military, I've never fought on the front lines, and I sure as hell have never been in a position where I had to make the conscious decision to leave my mortally wounded comrade behind. So, this was as raw as it could possibly be.

Immediately following Scott's tragic fall, I wanted to weep. I wanted to drop to my knees and cry out *"Why?"* But as much as I wanted to get to his side and bring him down the mountain, without the proper equipment, I just had no way of scaling down to him safely.

So, I made one of the most difficult and emotional decisions I've had to make in my life. I had to say goodbye. I had to put my entire focus on my own safety and on getting myself back down the hill.

The next two hours back down the west-facing side of Longs Peak were no cakewalk, either. Cold, terrified, and covered in snow, it took every ounce of concentration and determination I had to keep putting one foot in front of the other.

The way I've come to see it is, Scott passed away that morning doing something we both loved very much. I know he would not want the accident to prevent me from enjoying something we both love so dearly.

It took several years of healing before I felt ready. However, nearly three years to the day of his passing, in Scott's honor, I climbed my first 14er since the accident, with a trio of my buddies. We summitted Grays and Torreys—which were the first mountains I had climbed with Scott few years previously (second picture below). And as you can imagine, it was an emotionally rich and bittersweet moment.

Summit of Grays Peak, several years after Scott's passing. I'm on the far left.

Summit of Grays peak, a couple years before Scott's passing. I'm on the far right and Scott is in the grey hat and pants.

The reason I tell you this story is because I believe it likely mirrors a similar story of yours.

Your story may not be like mine; however, the way you and I have experienced pain and grief is no doubt remarkably similar. I empathize for what you've been through, whether it be loss of loved ones, sexual abuse, shame, trauma, or whatever the details of your pain. I'm writing this book to support your healing and integrating that part of yourself.

Because here's the interesting thing: not only is our pain and how we've experienced it likely very similar, but so is how our brains process it.

That thing between our ears? It's a "meaning-making machine." That's what it does best.

I'm confident, had I not been doing personal growth and self-discovery as intensely as I had been during the seven years prior to Scott's accident, I would not have handled that situation in the same manner.

That ability to take tragedy and decide how you want to respond to it rather than to react and find yourself at the bottom of a bottle—*that*, my brother, is pure personal power.

If you look up the definition of "power," this is what Merriam-Webster's definitions include:

1. ability to act or produce an effect;
2. possession of control, authority, or influence over others;
3. a controlling group;
4. physical might;
5. political control or influence

A big piece of this movement—of *Becoming a King in your life*—is about choosing to come from a place of personal power. Now, make no mistake: I am *not* talking about you asserting your power *over* others, possessing control by physical, mental, or emotional influences, or anything else in between.

Taking responsibility for *your* life and your beliefs and behaviors is all you have control over. And when those processes are in alignment with your heart, without ego, *that* is power.

I once saw a quote attributed to financial expert Dave Ramsey. In it, he said...

* Work is doing it.
* Discipline is doing it every day.
* Diligence is doing it well every day.

I see so many men who spend time each day talking shit, picking fights on social media, and shaking the proverbial hornet's nest of challenging people's opinions. But that's not confidence, courage, or love. It's the opposite of exhibiting personal power.

They may believe it is, but I don't. I believe power is owning your shit. Taking responsibility for *you*.

Power is being a man of your word. If you say you're going to do something, you fucking do it. Or you own the fact that you've broken your word and how you're committed to being in integrity going forward. Period.

Power is feeling fear and stepping through it, because you know it'll lead to growth. This isn't about ego and proving yourself. Stepping through your fear is about expansion. And becoming a fuller version of you.

Power is loving your significant other without expectation and, instead, exchanging expectation for appreciation.

Power is getting your shit done during the day so you can be at your kid's soccer game or be emotionally present to the needs of your significant other.

Power is being a participant in the lives of your wife and kids. Dirty dishes? Do them. Dirty diapers? Change them. Participate in the arena of life. Don't sit in the grandstands.

Power is keeping an open mind and being willing to take feedback. Your ego will often be your greatest nemesis. Learn to quiet it, and you become the master of your own destiny.

Power is taking care of yourself physically. You must take care of your own house, your temple, if you hope to have any sense of self-worth and self-esteem.

Power is apologizing when your ego would rather you be "right" than be happy.

Power is leaning into being vulnerable when you feel exposed and everything inside is screaming you to cover up, run away, or to be defensive. Leaders lead from the front lines, vulnerable to life's arrows.

Power can be a lot of different things. What it ultimately boils down to is taking personal responsibility for your thoughts, choices, and actions.

Brother, what if you're not willing to do this? Then there's no chance in hell you're ever going to become a King; a man worthy of emulation.

There are far too many examples of insecure, wounded, and sick men who use their "perceived power" to abuse, to take advantage of, and to inflict far greater pain on others than they are feeling within.

This is *not* the type of power I implore you to tap into.

In the following chapters, we'll explore how to embody the *correct* type of power. The kind that will help you live in abundance, show up for those you love, and *become a king*.

CHAPTER 1

The Addiction

"The biggest drug in our society is not alcohol or cocaine or pot. It's our problems. People are addicted to their problems, because it lets them escape their fears."

—Tony Robbins

HAD I BEEN EMOTIONALLY unfit on the day the world lost Scott, I would have likely blamed myself in some way. Frankly, it would have been a lot easier for me to say, because of the trauma from experiencing Scott's accident, that's why I turned to drugs, alcohol, or anything else I could get my hands on to dull away the pain.

That's the reason why I wanted you to know a portion of my story: not to impress you with how shitty an experience that was for me; but rather, to impress upon you how critical it is that you get emotionally fit. Because when you're not fit, it's so much easier to give up in those critical moments when life squeezes you.

And not only emotionally fit, but mentally, physically, relationally, financially, and spiritually fit.

Why is this so important a point that I begin my book this way? Let me give you an example.

If you had an extremely high level of physical fitness, what would you be capable of doing? Running marathons? Summiting mountains? Competing in the Olympics?

Compare that to the inverse. If you're physically exhausted, overweight, and always out of breath, how motivated would you feel to hike one of these mountains here in Colorado? Or to run around with your children in your backyard?

You're not going to feel up to it at all.

So, with greater physical fitness, you gain freedom.

Freedom of movement. Freedom to experience life from the top of the tallest mountains. And, with freedom in all areas of your life, the sky's the limit!

But physical freedom is just the beginning. What would you choose to do if you had financial freedom, relational freedom, spiritual freedom, emotional freedom, and time freedom?

All of that is available to each of us, as human beings. And it's *especially* so to you, because you're the type of man who has chosen to pick up a book like this.

And yet, are *most* men healthy, strong, purpose-driven, full of energy?

Are most men in a passionate relationship with their significant other, where they love each other deeply and desire to create win-wins for each other?

Do most men have a job, a career, or a business they love and can't wait to go to every day?

For most men, the answer is no.

Many men are addicted to control. They control their environment, they control their income, their appearance, their reputation, their emotions. For a lot of men, the idea of losing control is a sign of weakness.

I, too, believed this for a long time, until I began noticing that for men whom I experienced as Kings, the opposite was true. These men relinquished control of anything outside of them. They let go, and instead, they sought guidance. They allowed their emotions to pour out of them, and that's what made them passionate, courageous... human. It was because of their humility that they achieved true freedom from the shackles of mental, emotional, physical, relational, spiritual, and financial restraint.

And it's men like Scott, the few men who do experience freedom in all aspects of their lives, who show me—and you—that these freedoms are possible to achieve.

If you're anything like me, then you're not willing to accept a life that's "good enough" or simply "ordinary."

I want to support you in living life with a level of freedom that comes from achieving the status only a king can experience.

So, I implore you: don't fall victim to the trap of believing there will come a day when you've "arrived" and the work is complete. Truth is, the journey never ends.

And, honestly, thank God it doesn't! You know how boring life would get if you just got to "win" life like a game of Monopoly, and there weren't new levels to achieve?

I'm here to tell you—after having done "the work" for the last twelve years, the truth is *it's fucking difficult.*

What do I mean when I refer to "the work"?

I mean unlearning all the unhealthy coping behaviors you learned when you were little, healing your wounds, forgiving yourself and others, letting go of limiting beliefs and stories about who you are, understanding what you're capable of and NOT capable of, creating clarity around what your purpose is on this Earth, while creating a framework that supports maximum fulfillment in your daily life.

That's what I mean. Truthfully, for me personally, "the work" has been a lot more difficult than I ever imagined it would be. And chances are great that "doing the work" will also turn out to be a lot more difficult than you realize, too.

However, what's the alternative?

The more you continue to avoid the things that need to be confronted, and the more you've found your way into shitty and unhealthy coping mechanisms, like alcohol, video games, being a workaholic, Netflix binging, drugs, porn, sex, gambling, and other distractions (the list goes on and on), the bigger the mountain rises before you. And the more unfit you become.

Say you know you're physically out of shape. You feel fat and are physically hurting. However, rather than do something to make a positive change in your life, you stick your head even further into the sand, crack open another beer, grab a big bag of Doritos, and binge on Netflix yet again.

The way I see it is each of us has within us a worrier. And no, that isn't a typo. It's a part of us that stresses out over things that aren't within our control. A part of us that can get wrapped up in the state of the world to the point where we feel like everything around us is burning down.

And yet, on the other side of the coin, I also believe, within each of us, there is an inspiring leader for good! A warrior!

I don't care whether you identify yourself as male, female, straight, gay, or anything on the spectrums in between, each of us has a leader within us. And that leader has the power and courage to set in motion a chain of events that will powerfully and positively impact the world.

The challenge is often our traumas from our past will impede us from focusing on where we actually want to go in the future.

I'm a firm believer we, as a human race, are capable of things beyond our wildest dreams. The challenge is, more often than not, we're only as capable as our stories and limiting beliefs will allow.

In other words, what's the only reason you don't have what you want in life? *Because of a story you've been telling yourself about why you can't have it.*

Let that sink in for a moment.

The only reason you don't have whatever it is you want in this one-and-only life is because of a story you have created that tells you, for one reason or another, you can't have it.

The remedy?

Step 1: You must heal your past pains, trauma, and wounds. Without doing this, you will continually give away your personal power to either memories of the past or your anxiety about the future.

Step 2: You must get clear about what you choose your purpose and passion to be. It's only when you are able to be present in the here and now that you are able to find clarity around your life's purpose.

Step 3: You must establish the game of life for maximum fulfillment. It's not enough that you achieve or acquire a lot of things; you must learn to find fulfillment in the smallest of life's moments.

In short: To experience more, you've got to *be* more.

And that is what this book is about.

It's about building your life and becoming the King of your Kingdoms.

You must become the man you know you're capable of becoming in order to achieve all your hopes and dreams. And your hopes and dreams are what makes up your "Kingdoms."

You know as well as I there's no point in achieving great things in life if you're still a douchebag at the end of the day. To have achieved much and not be respected is a fate worse than death.

So, the next question is, how do you become a king? How do you want to be remembered? What type of lifestyle culture are you committed to creating?

It all starts with your uncompromising desire to no longer accept anything less than extraordinary in your life. It means you must raise your standards and live by a new code of conduct.

It's a way of being and a way of conducting your life that I will describe in far greater detail in the chapter entitled "The Code of Kings." But more on that later.

Updating Your Operating System

How often do you upgrade the operating system on your phone?

Since the iPhone first released in June 2007, how many upgrades has Apple made to their operating system?

Hundreds? Thousands?

According to the book, *Brilliant Babies, Powerful Adults* by John Mike, by the time you were four years old, fifty percent of your operating system (a.k.a. how you now ultimately think and behave as an adult) had already been installed. *Four fucking years old.* That blew my mind the first time I heard that!

From the ages of five to ten years old, the next thirty percent is installed. And from eleven to eighteen years old, another fifteen percent, for a total of ninety-five percent. That means most of who you'll be for the rest of your life, unless you choose to change it, has been established by the time you graduate high school.

It goes to show how vitally important those first years of life are for each of us.

And if your life in the time frame from birth to eighteen years old wasn't ideal, that means you've got some work to do.

The attitudes and emotions that determine your habits and behaviors dictate your result and ultimate outcome in life. In fact, ninety to ninety-five percent of our actions, behaviors, and thoughts come from subconscious drivers that are seeded in childhood. Clearly, they're massively impacted by what we experience as children and teenagers.

But hang on for a moment. Before I really dove headfirst into figuring out why my self-esteem was so shitty, I really didn't believe in any of this "self-help crap." If people said things like, "Well, perhaps your dad not being around for most of your life impacted how you are today," then my answer was to roll my eyes and shake my head.

Just the thought of attempting to connect all the dots in my past, in an effort to understand my life today, was so overwhelming, I would much rather continue living numb than open that can of worms.

The truth is, however, most of us had no choice or control over what we experienced as children. But we *do* have the power and responsibility to change the limiting beliefs and stories that are holding us back.

When *you* change, everything changes.

However, let me be clear: this book will not change you. *You* will change you.

If you read this book and do nothing, nothing will change. If you read this book and it motivates you to take a little bit of action, you will only move the needle a little bit.

How you will actually progress in life is by first learning the key strategies and mindset hacks discussed in this book. Then, through practice, repetition, and emotional commitment, you'll evolve into the man you are proud to be.

There are no quick fixes here. If you want to change your health and your body, it's not going to happen overnight.

So, if you're committed and ready to go, let's dive in.

CHAPTER 2

The Ordinary Man & His Wound

"If you are not willing to risk the unusual, you will have to settle for the ordinary."

—Jim Rohn

"There are wounds that never show on the body that are deeper and more hurtful than anything that bleeds."

—Laurell K. Hamilton

THE WAY I SEE IT is this: past generations of men did the best they could with the tools they had. In a lot of cases, it wasn't much. Chances are, your father and grandfather were raised to have an extremely unhealthy relationship with their emotions. Most men of their generation were.

However, at this time in human history, it's our great privilege and responsibility to upgrade our operating systems. To become our best versions of ourselves, you must first get your house in order before you become a mentor to others. If you don't, you just kick the can farther down the road.

By not stepping up, all you do as a man is take the shame, passivity, and deep pain you've inherited and willingly pay it forward to the next generation to deal with. By not stepping up, that will be your legacy.

And you know what I say to that?

Fuck that.

I am committed to being a springboard in every way, so future generations may stand on my shoulders to reach higher heights. Are you with me in this?

If we truly are to Become Kings, we must upgrade from "Ordinary" men to being "Extraordinary" men.

First, you must understand why so many men play it safe in life. Why are they living lives of quiet resignation that are anything by extraordinary?

The Wound and Masculinity

Every man carries with him a wound. In almost every man's case, the wound is given by his father, by his presence or lack thereof. And with every wound, there is a message. The message of the wound varies. However, when boiled down, many men live their lives questioning if they really have what it takes to be a man.

For me personally, I don't have many memories of my father. He was a workaholic, and even when he was around physically, I don't remember having many "present" moments with him. Instead of wanting to emulate my father, it was quite the opposite. I remember making a vow that I would never be like him and spent much of my teenage years trying to be exactly his opposite.

Without that strong male role model, I found myself gravitating toward male characters in the cartoons, TV shows, and movies of my childhood. Between age five and twelve years old, I spent countless hours alone in the woods, fighting imaginary battles like the ones I saw on television. In retrospect, I now understand, with each battle I fought in those woods, I attempted to answer an underlying question of whether I had what it took to be a hero and, in my mind, a man.

For the first thirty years of my life, I questioned if I was truly powerful, or if I was destined to be passive, weak, and incapable of rising to the occasion, should the moment arise when I would be called upon. I suffered from the imposter syndrome, living out this false sense of identity and feeling as though I was posing. My first marriage ended as a casualty of that inner battle.

I believe a lot of men can resonate with this deep-seated questioning of their masculinity. Why? Because, as I have learned, masculinity is not something we inherently get just for being born male. Masculinity is something granted to us by learning it from our father, from a man, or from a group of men. As well intentioned as women may be, it cannot be granted by women. Just as little girls could never learn how to become a woman from a man.

I grew up being recognized as a "momma's boy," and my mother would often refer to me as a "little angel." What I didn't realize was that, given the shortcomings of my father, my mother unintentionally sought to fill a void he had left open with me and my two brothers.

This created a massive opening for my wounding. For some men, they receive their wounding from their father overtly. Perhaps their father was emotionally, physically, or verbally abusive and communicated that they do not have what it takes to be a man. Other men receive their wound much more subtly. By having a passive or absent father, the childhood wounding of a boy can be less obvious and thus, harder to bring to the surface to heal as an adult.

Personally, when I think back on my childhood, I cannot think of a particular moment when I received my wound. Just having my father be absent, working all the time, was injury enough, because I never received his blessing. Perhaps you experienced the same thing? Desperately wanting to know what it means to be a man, wondering if you had what it takes, and instead all you heard was silence.

The byproduct of the wound being inflicted upon boys who eventually grow up to be men is they live by embracing their shadow masculine. Rather than be led by their own light, they fall victim to becoming either a "bad boy" or a "nice guy." "Bad boys" don't need anyone; they become violent, untrustworthy, and driven. "Nice guys" become people pleasers, passive, and spineless; they live lives by playing small.

The vast majority of these atrocities of pain are inflicted on the masses by wounded men who are living their lives through their shadow masculinity. And what I have found behind that mask of shadow masculinity, where a man lives his life posturing and pretending to be something he isn't, is a mask of anger.

However, as you keep digging, underneath all that anger is a masked man who is sad, lonely, depressed, and ashamed. And deeper one layer still, at the core of every wounded man, sits a scared little boy alone in a corner, hugging his knees and rocking back and forth, while tears stream down his face.

The Ordinary World

There I sat, zoning out, staring at the wall.

I glanced up at the clock, and an all too familiar sickening feeling went through my body. Had it seriously only been 15 minutes? I felt like this last hour of work had been the equivalent of three.

5 p.m. couldn't come soon enough. My daily twenty-minute commute had become the highlight of my day.

It was January 2010. Three months prior, I had been surprised with a gift ticket to a seminar called, "Unleash the Power Within." It was led by Tony Robbins, one of the leading personal-growth coaches in the world. And it had changed my life.

Since then, each day to and from work in the car, I'd been listening to one of his multiple programs on how I could improve my life. God knew, I needed every life hack I could get.

On this particular day, on my daily commute home, I got to thinking to myself, *I cannot continue to live this way—trading hours for dollars in a job I have no sense of purpose in. Being a man who has no passion. Something has got to change.*

What pained me the most was I had *no* recollection as to what I had accomplished that day. Like, I literally had no memory of what had gone on just hours prior.

I had been at work for nine hours of my life. And although my day had just ended, I couldn't for the life of me remember what I had accomplished. It was a blur of busywork with absolutely no significance.

How did it come to this?

Why was I so unhappy?

I mean, I had, on paper, everything I thought would equate to happiness. And yet, my heart was not full. Rather, it was numb.

I had hit a new low. I was emotionally flatlined. I was neither very excited or upset about anything in life. I was just fulfilling what I believed was my role as a husband and man, which was to work hard, provide, clock-in, and clock-out.

I felt no pull in life. No sense of purpose to anything beyond what I'd been taught to pursue.

I was deep in thought when the ideas just began to flood my mind.

Honestly, what I want is just to have my basic financial needs met. Then, I wish I could spend all my days just learning, pouring into myself, and becoming a better man. I wish I had something I was passionate about.

And that was precisely the problem.

As I sat there, I realized, even though I had achieved everything I always thought I wanted, I was deeply unfulfilled.

For most of my life, I had made getting married and settling down my end-all, be-all goal.

And yet, there I was thinking to myself, *Why am I so deeply unfulfilled? Do I even have what it takes to be happy? To be successful? To even feel like a man?*

There was a vast void inside me, one I worried I'd never be able to fill.

I had attempted to ignore and sweep these questions under the rug for the last several years. I had attempted to distract myself by becoming a workaholic, by traveling constantly, by training for a bodybuilding competition, by rehabbing my entire house, by starting an MBA program. Some of these things helped longer than others. However, at the end of the day, not a single one gave me what I was looking for.

What it would take me several years to come to discover was this: I'd been searching to reclaim my warrior's heart.

For most of human history, men have been warriors. The bloodline of warrior energy runs deep within each of us. It's that willingness to do whatever it takes to protect and provide for our loved ones, our family, and the things we hold closest to our hearts.

Over the last several centuries, men have lost their way. We no longer have initiation ceremonies that teach boys how to become men; men with a purpose beyond fulfilling only their own needs.

As a result, the "Ordinary Man" or "Nice Guy" was born. He's a man who damages himself, his loved ones, and the planet. He's a man who has lost his warrior heart and, in its place, is a void of self-preservation that cannot be filled.

If you're anything like me, there has always been a part of you that has longed to fight against the culture that coddles the ordinary man. Instead, I've sought something greater than myself.

I long for adventures in life.

However, there I sat, having just parked my car at home, feeling as hopeless and passionless as any man has ever felt. You see, my life really had little to do with the work, with the truck, with the house, or even my relationship.

There was something else out there. Something I knew I had to pursue. Something far more dangerous and risky; a goal I was equally excited to find, though I was fearful I'd come up empty-handed.

Who am I?

What is my purpose?

And the ever present wound, beckoning: Do I have what it takes?

Little did I know I was about to embark on the wildest, most rewarding adventure I could ever have imagined.

The Call to Adventure

Within a period of four years, from 2006-2010, everything I thought I knew—my way of life, those I had come to rely upon, everything I believed—all imploded and was gone.

In retrospect, I can now see it as a gift. A challenge, and a quest that had to be undertaken.

I was about to set off on a journey of becoming a congruent man, of becoming a king. And to do that, I had to find what set my heart on fire.

Bomb #1: They say things often come in threes. I found this to be true when I received the royal 1-2-3 punch that catapulted my life onto another whole level.

The first hit came on Sunday afternoon, October 15, 2006. I was on my way to visit my mom, who had been battling illness for the previous four or five months.

I was about ten minutes from her when my phone rang. It was my dad.

"Johnny, your mother has stopped breathing. She's gone. I'm sorry. The family is all here, so please just come home."

For me, whose upbringing to that point had been devoid of any major trauma, this was by far the first big record-scratch; the only real blow to the vision of how I foresaw life unfolding.

At the age of 61, my mom was gone.

Bomb #2: Fast-forward to the summer of 2009. At the age of twenty-nine, I had nearly three decades' worth of anger, resentment, and longing for a relationship with my father building within me. It culminated in me hitting a boiling point.

I remember it very vividly.

I called my oldest sister and said, "I'm so done with Dad. I want nothing to do with him anymore. I'm ready to divorce myself from having any interaction with him."

I remember feeling like he didn't even know me as a man.

Growing up, everything had always been about him. So much so that I seriously believed he cared more about his business than he did his own children.

I had been working for him at the family business for three years at that point, and what I longed for more than success was to see him take an interest in my development as his son.

I longed to feel special.

I longed to be respected.

I longed to be seen.

Hanging up with my sister that night, as far as I was concerned, I no longer had my mother or my father in my life.

An hour later, my phone rang. It was my sister again.

"Johnny...," she said, "I just got off the phone with Dad, and he wants to meet with you in his office tomorrow morning. Just trust me, don't do anything rash until you hear him out." The tone of her voice was different. It was worried, yet hesitant.

"Whatever. That's fine," I replied with a roll of my eyes.

I was done. And there wasn't anything he could say that would change anything. Or so I thought.

It was 10 the next morning when my dad popped his head into my office and asked if I would join him in his.

As I walked into his office, the energy felt tense and strangely unfamiliar.

He was at his desk, and as I sat down in front of him, he said, "Your sister tells me that you have something you may want to get off your chest."

With a sarcastic smile and subtle laugh, I said, "Yeah, just twenty-nine years' worth." Yet, I was thinking, *As if he cares.*

My toxicity toward this man was at an all-time high.

However, something was different about him that morning.

He sat in front of me on the other side of his desk, and for the first time in my life that I could remember, he was giving me his full attention.

What I had come to expect was quite different. Typically, over the course of an hour and a half, we would be interrupted a dozen times—by phone calls, text messages coming in on his Blackberry, important emails that needed a quick reply; essentially, a plethora of "urgent" tasks. Meaning, things I'd come to understand were more important than me and my needs.

Nonetheless, since I had nothing to lose (and he was offering me the opportunity to open a can of whoop-ass), I was going to let him have it.

Brother, I'll tell you what, I *unloaded* on my father.

Every grievance, everything he'd said to me that I would *never* say to a son of my own, every moment he'd missed out on to be a father, I let him know how severely he had failed me.

Something surprised me, however: the entire time, he didn't come to his own aid. He didn't attempt to rebut, rationalize, or justify any of his actions. He just calmly nodded in agreement and took it, square on the chin.

The only words he uttered over the course of an hour and a half were, "I understand. Is there anything else?"

I had never experienced my father's presence like I did that morning. Not once did he look at his phone, his watch, or at his computer. He gave me his undivided attention. And it wasn't until that ninety minutes was up that I finally had nothing else to say. I had no more ammunition left. I was spent.

At this point, when I said there was nothing more, I don't even remember what he said, and it didn't matter. I was already feeling 100% better than I had two hours earlier.

Who knew that expressing your raw and unfiltered emotions could be so healing? I felt as if an immense weight had been lifted off my shoulders and heart.

I was about ready to walk out of the office and write off the man when he said, "Now I have something I want to share with you." The expression on his face was somber.

Hesitantly and with curiosity, I said, "Sure. Shoot."

He turned his gaze down to the desk for what seemed like minutes until he finally looked up. With tears welling in his eyes, he opened his mouth to say something. Yet, nothing came out.

This went on for some time.

The more he attempted to speak, the more nothing came out. The only thing I noticed was that tears were streaming steadily down his cheeks now.

My mind ran in circles.

Oh shit, I thought. *Is he sick? Is he going to tell me that he, too, has cancer as my mother had, just after I completely unloaded the world's burdens upon him? Is he dying?*

Funny how our brains often go to the worst-case scenario.

"Dad..., whatever you have to tell me, you can tell me. It's okay."

My heart was already softening, and I felt empathy welling up in my throat. I had never seen my father like this, so emotional, so... vulnerable.

My eyes were fixed on him, hanging on his every failed attempt to say whatever he needed to say until the words finally came out.

"Johnny..., I'm gay."

For the second time in my life, I went into complete shock.

My first thought was, he had to be joking.

One thing I had come to know well about my father was he was a jokester. He loved to tease (and, in my case, the apple doesn't fall far from the tree).

My second thought was of immense gratitude that he wasn't sick.

Beyond that, I didn't think. I just opened my mouth and the words came straight from my heart...

"Dad, who you love is none of my business. You're still my dad, and being gay doesn't change the fact that I love you."

I could almost see what must have seemed like the weight of the world fall from his shoulders.

With tears still in his eyes and running down his face, he said, "Thank you, Johnny."

We stood up and hugged it out. That morning of being able to release a lifetime of resentment, coupled with his truest presence and vulnerability, changed my relationship with him from there on out.

Bomb #3: It was March 18, 2010. My flight had arrived on time. And as I walked off the plane, I almost threw up on the jetway.

My stomach was in knots more than it had ever been in my life, and the uncertainty of what was about to happen had me physically ill. Even more so since the conversation I'd had just forty-eight hours prior.

Her words were still echoing through my brain.

I was at a convention for work in Vegas. "Do you even want to be married to me still?" I'd asked.

I remember the out-of-body feeling and shock I felt when those words came out of my mouth unpremeditated.

I knew I was failing at being anywhere close to the husband I knew I had the potential to be. However, this was the largest wake-up call of them all.

The next forty-eight hours of my life, before walking off the jetway, were gut-wrenching. The not knowing, the silence, the lack of sleep... Anyone who has been through a similar experience knows the feeling.

So, as I turned the corner to the passenger pickup area to look for her car, I said a prayer that everything would unfold just as it should. And, little did I know, it would, just not how I'd imagined it.

Within five minutes, my biggest fear became a reality, as I realized a divorce was imminent.

Needless to say, the next six months were the worst of my entire life.

Not only because of how painful the feelings of broken trust, loss, and heartbreak were. Even more so because it was my first realization of my co-dependency, enmeshment, and childhood woundedness, which were impacting every part of my life.

Lesson: Looking back, I can see and acknowledge there were countless flaws and unhealed wounds that contributed to how I showed up in my life at that time.

However—something I've learned over the years, as a result of the heartache is: there are specific metrics; things I need to measure in order to know if my life is working or not. Those metrics can be applied to your life, as well.

What I learned from people who had an impact in my life—people like Tony Robbins, Lewis Howes, Christine Hassler, Brendan Burchard, Esther Perel, and countless others—is that our entire lives are guided, moment-by-moment, by the emotional state we are in.

For instance, if you're feeling frustrated, pissed off, and lonely, you're going to respond to others and events in your life in a completely different way than you would if you were feeling grateful, focused, and playful.

In fact, something I learned from lecturer, author and researcher, Dr. Joe Dispenza, is that, for most people, eighty to ninety percent of their thoughts are the same thoughts as the day before. What this amounts to is, if everything in your life and within your body stays the same, *YOU* stay the same.

CHAPTER 3

The Power of Emotional Fitness

"You have power over your mind, not outside events. Realize this, and you will find *strength*."

—Marcus Aurelius

Emotional State Management

HAVE YOU EVER GOTTEN really angry at someone who didn't deserve it? Only to realize later that you were *actually* angry at something *else* from earlier in the day? Something that overflowed into your interactions with an unsuspecting loved one?

It's happened to me on plenty of occasions.

It's a very clear example that illustrates the fact that, moment-to-moment, your life is controlled by the emotions you're feeling *in that moment*.

Another way of saying it is this: your life is controlled by the emotional state you're in.

On my podcast, I interviewed Ryan Michler, who is a husband, father, Iraqi Combat Veteran, and Founder of the Order of Man brand and podcast.

During our conversation, Ryan put his advice to men simply and powerfully: "Focus on the small things you can control and not on the big things you can't control. Those will work themselves out eventually."

Little did I know, for much of my life, as Ryan said, things would always work themselves out eventually. Instead, I remained unaware of how I could choose to control the emotions I was feeling.

When I was dating women in high school and college, I could be having a great day... until the point when one little comment made by my girlfriend would send me into a tailspin.

Similarly, when I was thirty years old and started my first business, I was living off revolving debt. So, whenever I received my credit card statement and saw I was $10,000+, $20,000+, $30,000+ in growing debt, the pressure I felt in my chest would lay me out for days.

I remember when the shift finally occurred. It was after months of this happening. I had just received my credit card statement in the mail.

As the envelope sat there, unopened, I stared at it on my kitchen table. I asked myself the simple question...

"Johnny, you're in a great mood right now. Your business is beginning to thrive and make money. You're giving back in a significant way. Are you really going to let black ink on a piece of paper completely rock your world? Are you going to give all your power away? Let a financial statement keep you from being happy today? Surrender your well-being to ink on a piece of paper?"

That was the beginning of my really starting to take responsibility for the emotional state I wanted to live in, day-to-day.

Because learning how to change—at-will—the emotions you're feeling... Being able to go from being angry, frustrated, and isolated to feeling centered, excited, driven or anything positive... *That* is going to move you forward in creating a better quality of life for you and others. It's a critical skill set for becoming a king.

A skill set you can learn!

Later in this book, we will dive into what controls those emotional states, long-term. Because how you're feeling in any given moment is determined by how you view the world.

So, ultimately, by the time you finish the book, you'll be able to measure various metrics to determine what needs to be changed in order to live happier and healthier. And if you're living unhealthily, you'll have the tools to know how to shift into taking back control at any moment.

Let me just mention something while we're on this topic. You'll want to highlight this and/or write it down in your notes...

Men who allow their emotional states to be dictated by their circumstances (i.e., whatever is happening around, and to them) will often look for pleasurable ways to escape the pain, when they're in it.

I specifically use the word "pleasure," as it often takes the form of vices, like alcohol, sex, drugs, gambling, food, gaming—you name it. Pleasure is always something found outside of you. And it's fleeting.

Happiness, on the other hand, comes from within you. And it is what lasts.

Not surprisingly, what people *really* want is happiness.

Think about it: whenever something amazing happens in your life, when you've learned of some incredible news, or you've accomplished something extraordinary, what's the first thing you want to do?

You want to share it with someone you love.

That's a good example of how happiness comes from within. Also, how it's magnified when you give and share it with others.

Compare that to pleasure. Pleasure, more times than not, is something you're looking to get because you're focused on your own needs.

Pleasure is a form of taking. Happiness is something that you instinctively want to give.

I'll tell you this right now: so many men are in search of things outside themselves, things they hope will bring them freedom.

When I achieve this, when I accomplish that, once I get that promotion, once I'm a millionaire, once I get that new house, once I can finally retire... Does any of that sound familiar?

So much of our lives is defined by looking to get something, which presupposes a belief that we are currently in lack, or scarcity.

Anytime you start a sentence with, "I want... X, Y, or Z," that tells your brain you want it because you do not have it.

Your life will never feel complete or free until you realize the answer has been, is, and always will be found within you. Not outside of you.

Everything you will ever need is, in fact, already inside you. The task is locating and recognizing it within.

Becoming a King is about your ability to live your life from a place of authenticity. A place where you *choose* to experience feeling extraordinary emotions each and every day. And you do it in such a way that, no matter what life throws at you, no matter the highs or lows, you remain in that extraordinary state of gratitude, bliss, and abundance.

That, my brother, is creating dominion over your life and its circumstances.

If that is all you were to get from this book, then the toil, sacrifice, and love I put into writing it will have been worth it.

The path to living in an extraordinary emotional state requires an extremely high level of emotional fitness.

It's not unlike being a professional athlete. You've got to have your mental and emotional inner game at an elite level.

So, how do you get there?

The first step is to recognize that what controls and determines the highs and lows of life is *your emotions*.

Have you ever experienced something right alongside someone else, and yet your experience and the meaning you associated with what happened differed drastically?

I was talking with a buddy who was telling me about a previous relationship he had been in, where this happened on a daily basis. He gave me permission to tell his story anonymously...

He met a woman. And, instantly, there was something special. Chemistry. The "X factor," as he referred to it.

He'd met this person the first time for coffee at one of his favorite spots, and an hour later, as he was walking to his car, he was so excited, he immediately called me to tell me about whom he had just met.

They began dating. For the first couple of weeks, he was smitten.

"I thought she was the one, man!" he told me, as he recalled their meeting with excitement in his eyes. "I mean, I didn't want to jump to conclusions prematurely. I just hadn't felt that way in a *long* time."

Everything was going great. That is, until he got assigned a huge project at work that demanded a ton of his time.

"Since that new work project, things have changed so much. I don't get it!" he told me one night as we were grabbing dinner.

"Tell me what's going on," I said.

"Well, I got that promotion. And along with it, more responsibility at work. Which unfortunately means, until the contract is complete, I have to put in a ton more hours. The day I found out, I excitedly called her to share the news, thinking she'd be psyched for me. Instead, she completely shut down."

"She just shut down? What do you mean?" I asked.

"Well, like, she just stopped talking. When we grabbed dinner that evening, she just stared at her food while she ate. I asked why she was upset. She didn't want to talk about it. You would have thought I had just told her one of her dogs died," he told me.

"What do you think happened?"

"I don't exactly know, man. I mean, during one of our first dates she told me she was really sensitive. However, this was the first time I had seen this side of her. Like a switch was completely turned off."

I scratched my head. "And is this the only time that's happened?"

"No, over these past few months, it's happened *all* the time now. When I'm in a relationship, I like to tease, be playful, and make jokes. I guess it's my way of flirting. And now she never laughs. She just scowls at me with such contempt, as though I were the worst human being on the planet. It makes me feel like I'm walking on eggshells with everything I say or do."

"Man, that's shitty, brother. What do your instincts tell you to do?"

"I honestly don't know. I've completely shut down around her, too, though. Because I feel like any joke I make is going to piss her off the rest of the day. Any feelings either of us had seem like distant memories. I'm really scared, because I feel as though we're in a tailspin, and I have no idea what to do to pull out of it."

I'm sad to say they broke up just a week after he and I had that conversation.

I tell the story because it's a great example of how our own personal psychology, beliefs, and values create a wide range of meaning that we then associate to things in our lives.

Just as we all have had a bad day at work and it's overflowed into our interactions with a friend or loved one (someone who had nothing to do with why we were upset), life's pain and trauma are the same way.

If you don't get to the source of the pain and heal it, it will leak into every crack and crevice of your life and all your interactions with people.

My buddy told me that, during the last conversation he had with her—when they were breaking up—she admitted she had been feeling resentful toward him about the big project and promotion he'd landed within the first two weeks of their dating.

She went on to tell him it had triggered in her feelings of abandonment; feelings she had experienced in previous relationships. She'd gotten really scared that my buddy was going to do what her previous boyfriends had done, which was to completely immerse himself in work and leave her emotionally starved.

So, you see, my buddy and his ex experienced the same event—his promotion—yet took completely different meanings from it. For him, he thought, "This is an amazing opportunity. I'm being rewarded!" While she felt, "Here we go again. He's going to choose work over me. This will end the same way as before. No man will ever choose me as #1. They're all the same."

The difference in how my buddy and his ex-girlfriend perceived the opportunity he'd gotten at work tainted the remainder of their interactions and ultimately led to the death of any possible love they had for each other.

Once she anchored a negative meaning to his promotion, it triggered a pattern of her emotions and a way of coping intended to protect her heart from being broken.

It was really sad to see my buddy go from feelings of falling in love to later telling me, "Johnny, it was the *most exhausting* relationship I've ever been a part of. I just don't get it. To go from feeling like I was falling in love with her to feel like she was sucking the life from me. I can't believe we didn't even make it ninety days."

It's sad. Because his ex-girlfriend was clearly triggered into a pattern of emotions that ultimately perpetuated a self-fulfilling prophecy of failed relationships for her.

"The hardest part," he recalled, "was that, the more I pushed for us both to work on healing, the more she said she was fine and that this was my fault. She wasn't willing to do the work. That's when I knew it was over."

It proved to be a very powerful learning experience for my buddy. I really appreciate him for allowing me to share this example.

Think about it this way: many of the emotions you experience today are actually just the byproduct of you being triggered by your past. If you have not done the work to move beyond your past traumas and hurts, chances are you'll continue living your life in reaction to whatever may trigger those painful emotions.

Like someone who can never say no to a dessert when it's offered to them, you, too, will feel completely out of control emotionally, because you're constantly being triggered. Essentially, you will be thinking and living in the past. This is why healing and integration are vitally important.

Once you're able to move beyond the emotions that are triggered by memories of pain and hurt, you will no longer experience the present or future through the lens of your past.

Only then, will you be able to see the potential of what your life as a King could truly be.

Forgiveness and Freedom

Have you ever injured yourself?

I certainly have. One of the nagging injuries I've experienced was when I gave myself a sports-related hernia early one morning at the gym, while attempting to set a new personal record on my squats. Bad form and a weak core led to a tear in my lower abdominal wall.

Did I do anything about it? Nah. I ignored it, thinking it would just go away. The hernia got so bad I couldn't work out or lift anything. I still continued to ignore it, dismiss it, and minimize the injury until it got so bad, I couldn't even carry my groceries inside from the car. That's when I knew surgery was imminent.

The surgery was very invasive into my lower abdominal area, but the recovery was even worse. Since this was the first major surgery of my life, I miscalculated how long it would take me to get back in shape. I began to accept I'd experience pain and loss of mobility for the rest of my life. At twelve months after surgery, when I found myself in my first yoga class, I couldn't do even do a plank. The pain was excruciating.

After a short stint of playing the victim, I began my research and came up with a rehab process based off various YouTube videos and blogs. Over the course of the next twelve months, I regained all my strength in my core, so I could do five-plus-minute planks and was stronger than ever. It only took twenty-four months, which, at the time, felt like an eternity.

What I've now come to understand is that surgery is only one step of the process. Properly rehabbing from it is just as important, if you want to be able to have a level of mobility and strength equal to what you once had.

Forgiveness is a very similar process. If there's anyone in your life whom you feel triggered by or have energy about anytime you think of them, then that's a signpost there's work to do. Otherwise, being hurt emotionally is like a physical wound. We often learn to live with it, however our quality of life is greatly inhibited.

A big part of your evolution as a man is in forgiving those who have hurt you, whether they're alive still or not. Just saying, "I forgive you," without doing the work to process and heal is like getting surgery without rehabilitation. Suppressing any unresolved hurt and anger will be a drain to your life of fulfillment.

Unlike the wound after my hernia surgery, the pain from abuse, trauma, abandonment, anger, and resentment is like a wound you cannot sew closed. Like the emotions I felt toward my father before I learned what he was going through, my childhood wound acted as if it was infected and was only getting worse with age.

Brother, this is why you must begin the process of forgiveness and healing. I can imagine, if you've been hurt beyond comprehension, you may not feel ready to go there, because you may think I'm asking you to let them off the hook for doing what they did or believe you'll have to invite them back into your life, but that's not what I'm asking of you.

Whether someone has done something unimaginable to you or you have done something you feel a tremendous amount of shame for, forgiveness is the path to sovereignty.

Just because you forgive someone doesn't mean you're required to let them back into your life, only to be hurt by them again. You are allowed to forgive and to move on. So, this is what I'd recommend, in order to process forgiveness:

1) First and foremost, you've got to acknowledge what has happened. When I watched *Leaving Neverland,* a documentary about two men who were sexually abused by Michael Jackson, the first step toward healing was the acknowledgment that they had been abused.

It wasn't until they both had children of their own and their sons were the same age as they were, when their abuse began with MJ, that they each realized how wrong the abuse had been. Likewise, if you're minimizing, dismissing, or justifying away your hurt, this most likely is contributing to your numbing or inability to feel emotions in life.

A big part of dealing with your pain is to stop lying to yourself that it's not a big deal. Stop pretending like it doesn't hurt. Dr. Joe Dispenza said, when you act like it didn't happen, it's as if your heart calcifies. It doesn't matter how long ago the wound was given, you have to acknowledge the hurt, otherwise you cannot forgive that which you haven't acknowledged.

How is it affecting you and your life today? How did it steal your light from you? What has it cost you? What have been the consequences of living with this pain or shame all your life? If you do not face the hurt, you will die from it. The only way to heal is to acknowledge and experience the hurt.

2) Secondly, you must open your heart to better understand where they (or you) were at, in life, at the time of the wounding.

For me, having my father open up and tell me he was gay allowed for room in my heart to better understand the context of my own wounding by him. This is not to say that, by understanding where they were in their lives, you give them a free pass or justify their (or your) actions.

Rather, it's to say that, with this greater context, you can have greater compassion that they were doing the best they could with the tools they had at the time. It does not negate the fact that you were wounded. Compassion and empathy are fertile ground for healing. It's only from this place of compassion that you can fully heal and forgive.

3) Last and most important, you must forfeit any rationale to seek revenge.

There are four warning signs of a dying relationship. Chances are good that you've gone through these four stages, if your heart is hardened. We will call them the Four Rs:

Initially, you'll feel some **resistance**, like an underlying sense that you know something isn't right. If you don't listen to that subtle feeling, you may then begin to feel **resentment** toward yourself or another person. As your wound continues to become infected, you'll then move into **rejection,** where you push them away or isolate yourself. It's only then that you would move into **repression** or **revenge**, where either you internalize the emotions or you seek to inflict the same pain you have experienced on someone else.

Only once you've moved through these three steps will you be ready to truly forgive and let go of the pain that has been tied to you. Without freeing your heart from this cage of repression or revenge, you will never be able to experience the full breadth of human emotion.

As you begin to forgive and feel again, part of building your Kingdom lifestyle is knowing what levers of emotion you must pull, in order to experience all that life has in store!

The Three Levers of Emotions

You know what's fascinating?

There are over 3,000 words in the English language that are used to express both positive and negative emotions. What's also fascinating is the average person thinks 60,000 to 70,000 thoughts per day. And yet, studies have shown that most people experience fewer than a dozen of these 3,000 emotions in a given week.

Of the roughly 65,000 daily thoughts, ninety percent of them are the same today as they were yesterday. So, if most of your thoughts are the exact same as they were yesterday, no wonder why you fall back into the same rut you've been in for years, no matter how hard you try. Upon learning this, it makes logical sense why change often feels terribly difficult to create.

And since emotions are the fuel that drive your life, do you think it'd be useful to find better ways to tap into a greater variety of them?

I know for myself, when there's anything I've been really driven to accomplish in life, it has always been fueled by emotions of excitement and enjoyment.

Emotional Fitness Exercise

To illustrate how important becoming emotionally fit is to your overall success and fulfillment in life, let me walk you through an exercise.

Positive emotions often felt by people include:

- ✓ Excitement
- ✓ Joy
- ✓ Optimism
- ✓ Ecstasy
- ✓ Resilience
- ✓ Anticipation
- ✓ Love
- ✓ Passion
- ✓ Determination, etc.

Negative emotions people regularly feel include:

- ✓ Anger
- ✓ Frustration
- ✓ Loneliness
- ✓ Nervousness
- ✓ Sadness
- ✓ Depression

- ✓ Stress
- ✓ Anxiety
- ✓ Shame
- ✓ Fear, etc.

What are the positive and negative emotions *you* experience on a consistent basis (i.e., at least once a week)? Write them down in the space below or in your notebook/journal. Then circle the three you feel most often in each list.

Positive Emotion:	**Negative Emotions:**
_____	_____
_____	_____
_____	_____
_____	_____
_____	_____
_____	_____
_____	_____
_____	_____
_____	_____
_____	_____
_____	_____

Now that you have your two lists, it's important for you to explore where these most frequent emotions originate.

I know, as a fellow man, this may not be something you've ever thought about. However, my thought is, if I can make logical sense of the root or cause of something, then I can also learn how to get a different result, if what I'm getting isn't what I want.

So, to get to the source of where our emotions originate within us, it's important to learn the three levers that control your ability to improve your level of emotional fitness.

Lever #1: Your Physiology—how you use your body, exercise, move, breathe, stand.

Changing your physiology and the way you use your body is the *fastest* way to change how you're feeling emotionally. In short, it's much easier to act your way into changing your thinking than it is to think your way into changing how you act.

If you've ever worked out before, I bet you've experienced walking into the gym when you're *not* feeling excited to be there, and yet, if you've pushed through, you always feel better after a workout than you did prior to starting.

And why is that? In large part, it's because a big component of expressing masculinity, whether you're male or female, is doing something rigorous. Lifting weights, doing manual labor, MMA, boxing, chopping wood—anything forceful will connect you with a deeper sense of your masculinity. Remember: it's the fastest way to change how you're feeling, if you're ever feeling down.

Lever #2: What you focus on is where your attention goes. And where your attention goes, your energy follows.

Simply put, if you focus on all the shit going on in your life, you'll feel more of it. For instance, I get physical therapy on a monthly basis, and my therapist likes to torture me with dry needling. If you don't know what dry needling is, it's an invasive procedure where a fine acupuncture needle is inserted into the skin and muscle to the point where the muscle contracts or spazzes and then relaxes. (If that doesn't make sense, just search YouTube for it.)

Point is, it can be extremely painful. So, I've noticed, if all I do is sit there and focus on the pain, it's *way* worse than if I have my phone with me and use it as a healthy distraction. If I'm watching something entertaining or working on my Spanish learning, both the pain and time go by a lot faster.

Life is like that, too. Whatever you put your focus on, good or bad, you will feel and magnify.

As I mentioned previously, if ninety percent of your 60,000 to 70,000 thoughts a day are the same today as they were yesterday and your thoughts control your behaviors, then your personality is a byproduct of your thoughts.

It's a slippery slope, though. If you're not intentional about what you focus on, it becomes really easy to allow all of life's distractions to keep you from moving forward with purpose.

This is why a vision of an improved life is vitally important. If you do not have a life vision that is greater than your present, your day-to-day will be driven by the memories, emotions, and feelings of the past. And the end result? Your future will be a repetition of your past. Aka *Ground Hog's Day*.

Lever #3: Language/Intent—The words you use, whether they're spoken or just thought, impact the intent and the meaning of your experience.

For instance, let's go back to my buddy's experience with his ex-girlfriend.

He was awarded an amazing opportunity at work. One he was *stoked* about. And yet, his girlfriend associated a completely different meaning from that experience by embellishing a memory from her past that reaffirmed the emotion of abandonment. For her, this pattern of thinking kept her in the past.

So, if you have a bad habit of not using your body regularly to stimulate feeling better, chances are good you also have a habit of focusing on things that are disempowering.

When you focus on things that aren't helpful, it often persuades you to use language that takes away your power, instead of taking responsibility for your life.

Life will have a completely different meaning if you don't actively and intentionally choose what emotional state you want to live in. This is why it's so important to exercise and eat right.

At times, men tend not to give enough credit to the importance of nutrient-dense food being the foundation to limitless energy and vitality. I often say this to fitness clients of mine: the quality of food you eat is directly tied to the quality of life you experience.

If you regularly eat shit food, you feel shitty. When you feel shitty, you look at life through a shitty lens. When you look at life through a shitty lens, your entire experience can be dismal.

On the other hand, what happens when you eat quality food? You feel good. Your outlook is good. So, what do you suppose happens to the energy you put out and, therefore, attract?

This is precisely why you must raise your standards. Raise the standards of what you're no longer willing to accept. Raise your standards around the quality of food you intake, the quality of friends you surround yourself with, the quality of your thoughts, and then you've got to fight.

Keep in mind that the Founding Fathers of the United States of America *declared* their freedom and *then* went to war. They weren't a free country when they signed the Declaration of Independence. They declared it and then fought with everything they had to win their freedom.

The approach to gaining your own freedom as a King during your one and precious life is no different. You must envision it, declare it, and then fight for it!

The Hero and the Humbled

When I was eleven years old, my little sister got a new kite and desperately wanted to fly it. She had already spent time running around the yard, exhausting herself in an attempt to get it aloft during a windless day.

Soon, with tears streaming down her cheeks, she begged me to help. Something welled up from within me, and my inner hero heeded her call.

I looked in her big hazel eyes and nodded. "Yes, Molly. Let's go fly that fucking kite!"

Okay, perhaps I didn't swear. But I figured all I needed was enough speed and momentum to get that sucker off the ground. Like my kid sister, I, too, exhausted myself for several minutes, running around the yard.

After several failed attempts, the world's greatest idea came to me. It was as though a lightning bolt came straight down and struck me!

If I get on my bike and ride down the hill, with enough speed, there's no way this kite won't soar high into the heavens. I'm going to make this the greatest day of my sister's life!

So, imagine this: like a great warrior on his noble steed, I stood in the center of the street at the top of our neighborhood hill. Strung out behind me was fifty yards of line, attached to my little sister's pink "Hello Kitty" kite.

I was about to charge down this hill with all my might and fury, becoming the world's greatest big brother, the likes of which the world would never see again.

"*READY?*" I yelled to her as she stood at the entrance of our driveway at the bottom of the hill.

Giving an enthusiastic thumbs up, she screamed back, "May the Gods shine upon you and show that bitch of a kite who's boss!"

Okay, so, once again, my innocent six-year-old sister may not have spoken those exact words aloud. Still, it makes for a much more dramatic scene, so let's just go with it okay? Shit.

I slammed my heel into my pedal as hard as I could, while screaming "*CHARRRRRRRGE!*" and off I went down that hill.

I had one hand on the handlebar and the other above my head, grasping that kite thread. That day, it very well could have been the same sword that William Wallace wielded in *Braveheart*.

I was in the midst of sibling glory. At least, until the stark reality of the situation came crashing down.

I rode downhill while simultaneously looking backward and over my shoulder at Hello Kitty. I watched as she whipped this way and that, struggling to believe in herself enough to soar into the sky.

And then it happened.

Envision this... A single column of light seemed to break through the clouds. It shone like a spotlight on the kite as she began to climb into the air. Higher and higher, she ducked and dodged...

Until that little kite made a beeline straight into a tree. Immediately, the string snapped.

Without hesitation, I slammed on the brakes.

My momentous scene of valor turned into me hurling—in what felt like slow motion—over my handlebars, string still clutched in hand, then skidding to a stop on the pavement on my back in the middle of the street, bike wheels still spinning.

After screaming in horror, Molly ran for the house and called for help.

Something fascinating happened to me at that moment. What I thought for sure would have brought tears of defeat, tears of shame and embarrassment, actually produced the opposite.

In agonizing pain, bloody and recovering from having the breath knocked from me, I began to laugh. I laughed and laughed all by myself, knocked flat in the middle of the street. Reason being, the moment I'd believed would bring a lifetime of glory actually brought an associated meaning that would impact me the rest of my life. One that I believed equated to my no longer being a boy.

For most of my young life, I had been ashamed whenever I cried. I remember thinking to myself that, of all the superheroes I loved and admired, none of them shed a tear when things didn't go their way.

Somewhere in those first twelve years of life, like the vast majority of boys, I learned to associate crying and being emotional with shame and weakness. In this moment, though, I reasoned that my pain of going into battle to help a loved one and getting wounded (while not crying) was a symbol of fledgling manhood. Since I grew up not having an elder male affirm that I did, in fact, have what it took to be a man, I inappropriately associated my laughter, instead of crying, as indicating I was now even closer to the stoic hero status I longed for.

It fits perfectly in line with what I was being taught by cartoons, superheroes, and movies about what it means to be a man. Being a man meant being in control. Emotionless. Stoic. A warrior, who—even with his guts hanging out—fights to the bitter end.

Don't get me wrong, there are times when I see the massive importance of pushing through pain. Of not giving up just because it gets hard. However, even now, that very rarely includes shoving down and suppressing what I'm feeling.

For much of my life (and perhaps for yours as well) I was taught that to express feeling negative emotions was weakness. The way I perceived it, even at a very young age, was emotions got in the way of achieving, of producing, and of winning.

To be successful, I needed to be level-headed and focused. To be respected, I had to show I was always in control, never losing myself to fits of anger or desperation.

I believed that negative emotions were bad and shouldn't be felt, while positive emotions were good and desirable. In junior high school, I was enamored by Michael Jordan and the Chicago Bulls. Jordan was the epitome of an alpha male to me. Powerful, dominant, always getting the better of his opponents by having a stronger psychology. Now, certainly, a lot of Michael's success came as a result of this approach to life; however, there's a cost to every action.

Having decided to take on the same type of stoic attitude in everything I did—athletics, relationships with girlfriends, work—I now recognize this: the pride I once felt for the wall I built in younger years, to protect my heart from feeling pain and shame? It ended up being the same impenetrable wall that kept me from feeling positive emotions, like joy, excitement, and passion. Instead, it left me emotionally flatlined. Without the emotion and the motivation, the drive I once had was no longer there.

Over my childhood years, the pain of failing brought so much inner turmoil that I avoided committing 100% of myself to most endeavors in life. With less than 100% commitment, not surprisingly, I often came up short in my ultimate outcome. And when I failed at something, I would shrug off my failure by rationalizing that it was the result of having not given my all. Had I done so, I assumed, I could have been successful. I played it off like I knew I could be successful, but I willingly chose not to give my all.

The crazy thing was, however, that even when I succeeded at something, I wrote it off as being a fluke. Over the years, each and every experience chipped away at my self-worth and self-esteem. When I was successful, I rationalized and dismissed it away as a fluke, and when I failed, it solidified a growing belief that I wasn't good enough.

It wasn't until I was twenty-nine years old that I learned that every so-called "negative emotion" we feel is accompanied by a message and a call to action. I realized that, while I was suppressing and avoiding feeling the pain of "negative" emotions, I was also missing the opportunity to learn the valuable lesson these emotions had to teach me.

With the help of my amazing coach, Christine Hassler, I have come to realize the impact of suppressing my anger, frustration, disappointment, shame, sadness, rage, and loneliness, rather than what I can learn when I sit and feel these emotions.

Little did I understand that, just like a pressure cooker, if the building steam wasn't released, I too would eventually explode. The long-term effects of suppressing my anger has led me to vacillate between emotional numbness and outright rage.

When doing my best to suppress my negative emotions, they'll still find their way to leak out in the form of judgment, criticism, irritability, nit-picking, being annoyed by people, apathy, and boredom with life. That's all suppressed anger leaking. If you don't get it out, my man, it's going to explode in dangerous ways.

If you can take what I'm about to share with you to heart, you can learn to catch yourself in the middle of feeling furious, frustrated, overwhelmed, ashamed, etc., and move through these emotions quickly. You'll do so after realizing what each of these negative emotions is really telling you, rather than live in those emotions for days and weeks.

CHAPTER 4

Fears & Limiting Beliefs

"Fear is the path to the **Dark Side**. Fear leads to anger, anger leads to hate, hate leads to suffering."

—Yoda

"So many of us choose our path out of fear disguised as practicality."

—Jim Carey

The Messages within the Mess

WHEN I FIRST LEARNED the concepts I'm about to share with you, I was floored. For so many years, I had done everything within my power to avoid "feeling" negatively.

Little did I know that within every mess, there is a message. There are "sign posts" that point us in the correct direction.

So, rather than burying my feelings deep down inside—only to let them fester, grow, and eventually bust out of me—I came to realize the best time to handle any uncomfortable emotion is when I first begin to feel it. And I recommend you do the same.

When I was little, I remember my mom had this pressure cooker that would chatter and spit whenever the pressure inside the pot needed to be released. This emotional process is meant to do the same thing.

The key is to find healthy ways of releasing the pressure of building emotions prior to "popping off" and doing or saying something you'll regret later. Men often bounce between low and high levels of energetic emotion. For instance, we can swing from depressed (low energy) to anger or rage (high energy).

At the end of the day, there are ten primary emotions. These are feelings that, if not handled when they're small, can grow into ugly beasts—creatures with the power to control your thoughts and behaviors.

1. **LONELINESS:** One of the more common emotions men tell me they feel is *loneliness*. The message within the mess of loneliness is that you need to feel connected with others. The key is to not fall into the trap of thinking the only solution to loneliness is sexual intimacy. Have you ever been sexually intimate with someone and, afterward, still felt a deep sense of loneliness?

The solution is simpler than we often realize. All it requires is for you to reach out to someone and make a connection. Perhaps to a loved one, a friend, or possibly even a stranger. The good thing this message is telling you is that you really do need people in your life. You just need to identify what kind of connection you really desire—whether it's for someone to listen, to talk to, to laugh with, or to be romantic with.

2. **FRUSTRATION:** One of the emotions you may feel consistently throughout your day-to-day life is *frustration*. The message within the mess of frustration may actually make you excited, because we often feel this way when our brains believe something is within the realm of possibility.

The solution to handling frustration is to change your perspective and get creative about how else you could accomplish the task at hand. Perhaps you could ask a friend, hire a mentor who has a proven track record of results in this area, and/or get curious as to what new actions you could take to achieve the desired result.

3. ANGER: Another extremely common emotion men feel is *anger*. Whether you're a little pissed off, resentful, or full-on enraged, the message within this mess is you or someone else has violated an important guideline or standard that you uphold for your life.

When I talk of guidelines, I mean, whether you realize it or not, you have beliefs about what must happen in order for you to allow yourself to feel good about a given circumstance. Chances are extremely high, if you're often unhappy, it's because you've structured your life in a way that your happiness is dependent upon something you cannot control.

For instance: for a long time, I defined my self-worth by the affirmation I received from women. Whether it was my mom, my female school teachers, or those I was in romantic relationships with, it wasn't long before I began to experience the fact that there are just days when, no matter what I did, she wouldn't be a happy camper.

Which in turn meant I, too, was having a horrible day.

What I had to learn to do was simple. I had to decide I was not going to give away my power to enjoy my day. Enjoy an event, a challenge, and whatever came to me, no matter what happened. Truth is, I had a hard time doing this at first. It was difficult, until I recalibrated my self-worth to be determined by what I felt about myself and my sense of integrity—*rather than* defining it based on my attempt or ability to control someone's emotions (which, of course, were not within my control).

Target Focus Training creator and guest on my podcast, Tim Larkin, said, "By creating a healthy relationship with your aggression, you're more likely to react with power, clarity, and compassion."

The solution to dealing with anger when you begin to feel it is to recognize whether or not you may have misinterpreted a situation. And the best way I've found to go about doing this is to ask continuously, "What else could this mean?"

By asking, "What else could this mean?" I open myself up to other possibilities. Maybe the person in question is not standing me up. Perhaps—God forbid—they were in an accident. And it could be what they need right now is not my anger. It's possible they need my prayers.

For instance, if you're angry, it helps to change your perception of what's going on. The fastest way to do this is by asking a better set of questions. Questions such as, "What can I learn from this?" Or, "Is it true this person really cares for me?" "Perhaps there's a very logical reason for why this has happened... What could it be?" Lastly, recognize that, even if someone broke one of your rules, perhaps your rules suck and need to be reworked.

4. DISCOMFORT: One of the lowest, most underlying, nagging emotions men feel is *discomfort*. The message within the mess of discomfort is that something is off.

So, whether you feel bored, uneasy, unnerved, embarrassed, or impatient, chances are good that the solution requires you get a greater level of clarity on whatever it is you want. Rather than distracting yourself and ignoring this underlying feeling, sit down, breathe, and question what it is that is really bothering you. And once you have greater clarity, taking action in a different manner will often help alleviate feelings of discomfort.

5. HURT: On the other side of the spectrum of discomfort is *hurt*. Have you ever lashed out at someone undeserving of your anger just because you were hurt from something earlier in the day?

The message within the mess of hurt is that you are feeling a sense of loss. It's the acknowledgement you had an expectation that wasn't met. You expected someone would follow through or something would happen. And when it didn't, your sense of loss created a feeling of hurt.

The solution to this is to take a step back emotionally. To recognize there may not, in fact, have been a loss of anything. Again, perhaps by asking the question, "What else could this mean?" you could recognize that whatever happened was not an intentional action on their part. And the best way to lower the energy of feeling hurt is to go to the individual by whom you feel hurt and maturely communicate with them about how you're feeling.

6. **DISAPPOINTMENT:** A close cousin to hurt is the feeling of *disappointment*. If you don't nip that one in the bud quickly, it can grow into an extremely destructive monster.

The message within the mess of disappointment is similar to hurt. Because there's an expectation that you realize isn't going to happen, you feel "let down." For instance, I felt disappointed for a long time that I didn't have a childhood with a father who was more present than mine was. I felt hurt he didn't seem to care (which wasn't true, but that was the meaning I created), and I was disappointed that other friends of mine had more present fathers. I had an expectation my father should have been different from how he was.

The solution is you need to take a breath and recognize whether or not your expectation is unrealistic. Perhaps you believe you should already have heard back from an associate about a decision they're making. Instead, realize that not knowing doesn't mean it is necessarily a no. Be patient, and go back to what you ultimately wanted out of the situation. Ask yourself if there is a better, more effective way of achieving it.

7. **GUILT:** Over the years, I've often caught myself feeling a sense of *guilt*. When it comes to guilt, the message within the mess communicated to me was that I had violated my own standards.

For instance, when I was in third grade, a girl told me she liked me and explicitly told me not to tell anyone, as she wanted it to be our secret. So, what did I do? I was so excited, I immediately went and told three of my guy friends. And while I was telling them, she walked around the corner and heard me.

Even as a third grader, I felt horrible. I had betrayed her trust and felt so much guilt. Had I known the solution to alleviating guilt, I would have taken responsibility immediately and acknowledged how I'd broken my word. And then I would have communicated to her that I was committed to ensuring it will never happen again.

8. **INADEQUACY:** Professor and motivational speaker Brené Brown talks a lot about shame. She speaks about the fact that what's underneath shame is often a feeling of *inadequacy*. It's a feeling of unworthiness and can be extremely destructive. However, the message within the mess of inadequacy is that you're not yet skilled enough to achieve the desired result.

Sometimes, this is because you may lack the skills, strategies, or tools. Sometimes you just lack the confidence. Either way, the truth is not that you're inadequate. The solution is that you just need to change your perception of what you actually need to learn. Inadequacy is not a permanent state of hopelessness, unless you believe it to be true. Instead, find yourself a mentor, coach, or professional who can help you achieve the desired result in less time.

9. **OVERWHELM:** Another of the more commonly felt emotions today, one that creates the most drama, is *overwhelm*—in essence, being overloaded with things to be done. Those feelings of overwhelm often lead to further emotions of helplessness, grief, and depression.

The message within the mess of overwhelm is you're attempting to take on too much in the current moment, along with an expectation that everything must be accomplished immediately.

The solution is to determine what the "one thing" is that's *most* important to focus on doing. Then, continue the process of prioritizing in order of importance, whatever else you need to get accomplished. And once your prioritization list is complete, just start work on that most important thing and do it until you get it done.

10. FEAR: At the end of the day, all of our challenges in life boil down to one thing: what we *fear*. The message within the mess of fear is that we anticipate something will happen soon, so we must be prepared. However, most men will either downplay their fears or they'll stew in them without doing anything to alleviate them.

The solution to fear is to identify what you must do to prepare yourself for whatever you believe is coming. You can do that by taking action rather than sitting in fear.

Right on! So those are the most common emotions we feel as men, and the ones we often suppress or bury. What I recommend is, if you haven't already, read back through this section several times, and underline whatever sticks out to you as most relevant.

★ I recommend you take whichever of these ten are your top-three most commonly felt emotions, and write them out on index cards to keep with you. Write out the emotion at the top, the message it's telling you, and then the solution to move yourself out of feeling it. Keep them on you or in your car. (Personally, I have found myself getting angry at random times when I'm driving, so I find that beneficial.)

Taking the time to truly acknowledge what you're feeling—then to understand what that emotion is telling you and take action to remedy it—is the definition of someone who is emotionally fit.

This won't be easy. It will take time. However, it is what separates the men from the boys.

Refusal of the Call

I'll never forget one of the toughest days of my life...

I had decided to be out of the apartment for a couple hours, while the ex-wife and her mom packed up and moved out her stuff.

When I returned after they had left, I walked in the front door to see a house that looked nothing like it had just a few hours earlier. Even though I was well aware of what I was walking into, it was still shocking.

As I stood there in the hallway, the heaviness of reality began to sink in. I looked at a wall in the dining room that once was covered with dozens of framed photos of our friends, family, and our memories together. Now, all that was left were six photos of our wedding day. Apart from that, just empty nails protruding from the wall.

That's when I lost it and completely broke down. Like, ugly cried. My worst fear had become my reality. The very thing I grew up believing I'd always wanted—a wife and a future family—was gone.

And the icing? I had spent the majority of my life attempting to fake it 'til I made it. I suffered massively from impostor syndrome, and it finally felt like it had caught up to me.

I walked to the big windows of the family room and peered out at the pouring rain. It was coming down in torrents, like God was crying as hard as I was, out of shame, over the man I had become.

I had nothing but questions at that moment.

"Why?"

"Why did this happen?"

"Why did she leave?"

"How did I let it get to this point?"

It was at this moment that something I remembered having learned at a recent Tony Robbins seminar popped into my mind.

Questions You Ask Yourself

"The quality of your life is directly proportional to the quality of questions you ask yourself."

—Tony Robbins

Said another way: what you feel is determined by your focus, which is the result of the questions you ask yourself.

There I stood, having what seemed like a competition with God to see who could cry harder, asking questions that made me feel more and more like a fucking victim.

Let me tell you this right now: when you ask yourself shitty questions, you're going to get shitty answers.

How do you think my brain was answering those questions I was asking?

"Why did she leave?" *Because you minimized and diminished her feelings on a routine basis, you piece of shit!*

"Why have I failed as a husband and man?" *Because you never had any empowering male role models to teach you how a man is supposed to show up.*

"How did it get to this point?" *It got to this point because you didn't pay attention. You buried your head in the sand. You became a workaholic and took her for granted. You've finally gotten what you had coming, because you're never going to be good enough, and you will never be loved like that again.*

I was letting the victim mentality and the self-deprecating voice in my head run the show.

At that moment, I was hitting a new rock bottom. At that moment, I had never hurt as badly, nor wanted out of the pain as much as I did right then.

I remember thinking to myself, *How could you blame her? I wouldn't have wanted to remain married to that man, either.*

And then it happened again. The same quote popped into my mind...

"The quality of your life is directly proportional to the quality of questions you ask yourself."

This was a defining moment. Because at this point, I realized I had what seemed like only two options:

1.) Continue down this road of pouring salt into my own wounds (and who knew where that would take me...)

OR...

2.) I could take my power back and stop shitting on myself emotionally.

The next thought was, *If the questions I ask myself determine what I focus on, then what would be some better-quality questions?*

And the first one that popped into my brain was this:

Johnny, if you were currently writing the screenplay of a movie about your life, how could this moment be, when the music changes and it becomes the catalyst to when the warrior sets off on a greater trajectory for his life?

I'm not shitting you: that's literally the question that popped into my head. And the second question I followed it up with?

Okay, clearly the life I built for myself was a life neither she nor I wanted. So, what is it I REALLY should focus on now?

And the answer startled me.

A voice spoke a single word into my mind. And it was a voice that was strangely familiar and unfamiliar at the same time.

The voice was not mine, which made it unfamiliar. And yet, there was a peaceful resonance to it that made me feel safe within it.

It spoke to me. And it said, simply, "*Give.*"

I remember questioning it again. "Give?"

One more time the voice spoke to me in my head. "*Give!*" it said.

What do I have to give? I thought.

I was seriously at a loss. I sat there in front of the windows, watching the rain, but at least no longer bawling my eyes out. And as I watched it pour, I wracked my brain as to what I had the capacity to give.

And I'll tell you what, brother. If you're really hurting right now in your life, as you're reading this, ask yourself just as I did, *what can you give*? Especially when you feel like you've got nothing. That's really scary.

Still, it's amazing how quickly a question of that quality gets you out of your own victim story and into a place of narrowing your attention to action that will uplift others.

Our Greatest Fears

Over the course of the next three months, I wrestled with my greatest fears.

I wish I could say that having heard a voice in my head instructing me to "give" made everything become crystal clear, but it didn't. I was still living in massive resistance to how my life was playing out, and I was extremely scared.

The best thing I did for myself over the course of those first ninety days alone was to hire a coach.

I cannot imagine what he must have thought about me. Week after week, we'd have our coaching calls, and there was very little forward progress.

I was stuck in this vicious crazy figure-eight, where I'd swing from feelings of being a complete victim, hopeless and helpless. Then I'd swing to rage and anger, unable to understand how I had gotten to where I was. I desperately wanted out.

Believe it or not, something my coach drilled into me was, no matter what, we all have the same two fears when we distill everything down to their roots.

We'll get to that in a second. First, we had to do the work. So, we talked about *all* of my fears.

I could feel I was being called to step up; to become a *much* bigger version of the man who had shown up thus far in my life. Still, I was scared. And what was I scared of?

- More failure.
- Rejection in dating again.
- Never finding love and being alone.
- Never having a family and raising amazing children.
- Not knowing what to do with my life.
- What people were thinking of me.
- Raising the bar on my life, only to fail once again.
- Confirming a belief that I was broken and unfixable.

I was steeping in my fears at that time in my life. And I could no longer avoid, numb away, or distract myself from them.

The truth I believed was—at the end of the day—I didn't have what it would take to become a man I could be proud of. I was scared of getting to the end of my life, looking back, and seeing that I had *so* much untapped potential that had been left deeply hidden within myself.

What my coach worked me through was a direct process. He kept asking, "And if that happened, what would it mean?"

I wasn't sure what he meant, so he pressed on.

"Johnny, what would it mean if you raised your standards in life, only to fail again at your next relationship, your next business venture, etc.?"

I replied, "Well, if that happened, I think it would solidify the fear that I'll never have what it takes to be great, and I'll end up alone."

"*Exactly!*" He yelled. "You see, Johnny, all of our fears boil down to the same two things. And those two are, first, that we're *not enough*. And if we're not enough, our even deeper, second fear is that we *won't be loved.*"

My mind was blown. The more I searched, the more his words resonated.

At the root of my fears, of his fears, of your fears as you read this book, is that we worry we won't be enough. That we won't measure up. That we don't have what it takes to be great.

And if we don't have what it takes to be great, then we're nothing special. And if we're nothing special, our lives don't have any meaning. Thus, why then are we even here?

That's what it all comes down to.

Do our lives have any greater purpose than to be born, live a life, trading hours for dollars, only to die seventy to ninety years later?

It was so simple. And yet, so clear.

So, I began thinking back over my experiences in life…

My greatest fear in my marriage was to allow it to become a relationship like my parents' relationship. If I were to allow *that* to happen, then I feared not being worthy of love.

The way I saw it at the time was my divorce confirmed that my fear was true.

However, what was actually *true was whatever I focused on was what I felt, whether it was true or not.*

And since I had spent so much of my life focusing on a lie, on my fears, then I was experiencing them as if they *were* true.

Over the years, I was taught that *fear* could be summed up as an acronym...

F.E.A.R. = **F**alse **E**vidence **A**ppearing **R**eal.

Fear is what dictated every choice in my life for a long time. The fallacy of this habit is...

Decisions made from fear are never the right decisions.

Having said that, I believe there's a reason why our paths have crossed. I have a belief you and I are much more similar than we are different. Even though your stories aren't mine and vice-versa, I believe what drives us as men is identical.

Strategy. Story. State

Now, more than ten years later, the answer seems obvious. However, at the time, I was attempting to come up with answers to a valuable question. Specifically: "What do I have to offer the world?" when I was in the worst emotional state I had ever been in.

What I have learned is that this is a very common mistake most men make.

To illustrate this better, let's pretend you really want to lose weight and create healthier lifestyle habits.

There is a three-step process that men typically walk themselves through, when creating change. Often, when men decide to finally make a change to their health, they first begin by focusing on questions having to do with their...

1. **STRATEGY:** They immediately go to the question, "Well, how do I do it? How do I lose weight, and should I join a gym? Or what type of diet should I begin?"

For most people I've worked with over the last decade around losing weight, it's something they've attempted in the past and failed at achieving their goal. The challenge when that happens is that it's easy to form underlying limiting beliefs, as well as a disempowering...

2. **STORY:** Having attempted (and failed) to change their lifestyle and lose weight multiple times, some men have a limiting belief that supports a story. Such as: "You've tried losing weight plenty of times, and it's never worked long-term. Why do you think it's actually going to work this time? Stop kidding yourself!"

This type of story—one of limiting beliefs—is a typical foundation that puts these men into a negative emotional...

3. **STATE:** And when you have a crappy, disempowering story like that, chances are very low you're going to get excited for very long. You may get motivated for a few days or a couple weeks at best, but what's more likely to happen is this: with an ineffective strategy, story, and emotional state, those unhealthy lifestyle habits you've been practicing will continue to be your active way of coping, by numbing away that pain.

So, here's my most important of all ninja adaptations.

You've got to flip this script. Instead of starting with first asking "how" something will be done, you must instead begin with changing your emotional state.

Why? Because the emotional *state* you're in controls the *story* you tell yourself. And the *story* you tell yourself controls the *strategy* you come up with for how to accomplish something.

Follow me on this...

Step 1: Get into a Powerfully Positive Emotional State.

Consider your history. Chances are, you always come up with a lousy story when you're in a crappy emotional state.

I bet you've experienced feeling tons better when you walk out of the gym than when you initially walked in, and the same holds true for how you must approach life. By intentionally putting yourself in a positive emotional state, you'll greatly impact the story you come up with. When you positively move your body, which is the fastest way to change your emotional state, you'll be in a better mood.

Remember when we talked about how much easier it is to act yourself into changing your thinking than it is to think yourself into changing how you act? The same principle applies here.

When you're in a better mood, you can...

Step 2: Create an Empowering Story.

When you're feeling strong, confident, and positive, the story you will come up with to lose the weight and change your lifestyle habits once and for all will be told with far greater certainty. And creating that level of absolute certainty is instrumental. Otherwise, you can fall victim to that little voice in your head that undermines your sense of self-worth.

Just be careful, though, you don't fall victim to the thought that you're just pulling the wool over your own eyes. A limiting belief, when challenged, will dig in its heels in resistance. The truth is you can believe your limiting story or believe an empowering one. Rather than give way to allowing your negative, disempowered stories to play out, you *MUST* create a brighter story and vision of the future. Once you have this, you'll be able to...

Step 3: Create a Strategy with Certainty

With those two pieces firmly in place, where your physiology *and* emotional state are centered and powerful, the story of how you're going to lose weight and make lasting lifestyle changes will be more congruent.

When you align your body, your emotions, and your beliefs, the "how-to" path to creating whatever you want in life—big or small—will unveil itself to you.

Does this make sense?

This is why it's so important to be intentional about putting yourself into an effective emotional state. Doing this impacts every aspect of your day-to-day, moment-to-moment experience.

Like we talked about earlier: have you ever snapped and gotten really angry at someone who had nothing to do with why you were initially upset?

We all have.

That's a good example of how, when you're in a lousy emotional state, you treat yourself and others unkindly.

On the other hand, when you're in a really happy and excited emotional state, how much fun are you to be around?

This is why I highly recommend having powerful evening and morning rituals that intentionally put you in powerful and positive emotional states to end and begin your day.

"Okay, Johnny," I can hear you thinking. "That all makes sense theoretically. However, how am I supposed to implement that into my everyday life?"

I'm grateful for that question, as I realize it can be an extremely scary and dark time. Especially when you know you're in a downward slide mentally, emotionally, and physically, without any end in sight.

The first step to creating physical freedom and emotional fitness without any of the overwhelm, deprivation, or burnout begins with digging into your story.

Changing Your Story

When you look at your *State, Story,* and *Strategy*, both your emotional state and the strategy you use can be effortlessly changed in a moment.

That said, when it comes to your story, it's those unquestioned limiting beliefs that cause stress that you've *got* to question.

Remember: our limiting beliefs are just stories we have about ourselves, about others, and about how the world works. And they're all based on what we focus on.

As *Secrets of the Millionaire Mind* author, T. Harv Eker, summarizes it, "Where your attention goes, energy flows, and results show."

The crazy thing is our brains will manipulate what we see in order for it to be right.

For instance, if you think someone is an asshole, he could do the most thoughtful thing, and you'd still find something within his character to question his integrity and justify knowing he's an asshole.

However, if you love someone, and they do something horrible? You'll think to yourself, *Oh, they're probably just having a bad day.*

You see what I mean?

What controls our emotional state is our blueprint for how we view the world. That blueprint can be dialed up—or down—depending on various metrics, to determine if our living is healthy, or unhealthy.

So, if you haven't been happy, then we need to take a closer look at the following metrics. That way, we can better align your behavior and experience with what you want to create in your life.

This blueprint of how we view the world boils down to three dials:

Dial #1: How we're getting our needs met.

Dial #2: The art and science of living life on your terms.

Dial #3: Decisions.

Think about it this way...

With Dial #1, getting clear on what your focus is in life determines whether your life will be an example worth emulating or, worse, a warning of what *not* to become.

Dial #2 has everything to do with learning how to create incredible results in your life, while ensuring you're happy with your life along the way.

And with Dial #3, you must learn to make wise decisions with the choices you are given; otherwise, you can easily find yourself in a death spiral.

CHAPTER 5

The Target

"The odds of hitting your target go up dramatically when you aim at it."

—Mal Pancoast

EVER SINCE I CAN remember, I have been extremely aware of people, situations, and emotions around me. As the middle child of five kids, I had a unique perspective. I was always able to feel what it was like to be a younger sibling and also to feel what it was like to be an older sibling. I often sat back and took in everything around me. My other siblings, my parents, life. I soaked it up.

I was fascinated from a very young age about why people do what they do. So, perhaps not surprisingly, my initiation into reading personal improvement books started early, as well.

Since those impressionable teenage years, I've learned that, as human beings, we are built so much more alike than we are different. The only difference between you and me is our sense of identity. And that sense of identity is shaped and formed by what we aim at and value in our lives.

This is precisely why it is *so* important, if you're truly determined to change your life and tap into your greatest potential, you must learn to choose what you want in life intentionally.

How is this done exactly?

Dial #1: Your 6 Human Needs

The first-ever Tony Robbins event I attended was in Chicago, in October 2009. I went into the event not knowing what to expect. On the first day of the four-day event, I experienced some of my life's biggest "ah-ha" moments. One of the *very* largest was when Tony explained the six human needs to the crowd of nearly 5,000 attendees.

He went on to explain that all human beings—whether they were sitting there in that convention center or were past ancestors of ours from 2,000+ years ago—all had the same six human needs in common.

He went on to say that every love song, every war, every culture, basically anything that has been touched and impacted by our human race has been driven by human beings who sought to fulfill these six human needs in either constructive, destructive, or neutral ways.

Given that I was driven from a very young age to better understand why we, as human beings, do what we do, I was riveted. Here, within the first couple hours of the event, Robbins had laid it out in simple-to-understand language. And my mind was blown.

He went on to say that people have four primary needs:

* Certainty
* Uncertainty
* Significance
* Love/Connection

Also, two spiritual needs:

* Growth
* Contribution

I'll quickly explain each human need...

1) Certainty: This is one of our most primal needs. Centuries ago, this would show up as our need for shelter, warmth, safety, food, and water. With those primal needs now for granted in first-world countries, our need for certainty has evolved into our need for having a good job, a good degree, a safe neighborhood, money to pay the bills, a roof over our heads, our need to be certain of being loved, and the ability to live a certain quality of life.

2) Uncertainty: You might think this is a typo, because how could we as humans have paradoxically opposing needs? However, stay with me on this. Our need for uncertainty shows up in our desire for variety, adventure, spontaneity, romance, and surprises. We like the good forms of uncertainty, whereas we hate the bad forms, which might be a large bill that appears in the mail, something that breaks unexpectedly and needs to be fixed, confrontation in your relationship, or being diagnosed with a disease.

3) Significance: We all have a need to feel special, of worth, unique, and like we're valued for who we are. People may fulfill their need for significance by wearing flashy suits or buying expensive cars, boats, jets, etc. They can also fulfill their need of significance by being altruistic. Some people are the most significant because their problems are worse than yours. Others fulfill their need for significance by being more spiritual and self-righteous than you. People will find a wide array of constructive, destructive. or neutral ways to differentiate themselves as being significant.

4) Love/Connection: This one is pretty self-explanatory, as we all have a need to feel we're loved and to love others. We want to feel connected to others, our community, the planet. In many relationships where the love has faded, we may settle for the breadcrumbs of connection by way of raising children, traveling, eating—anything that will allow us at least to feel connected to someone or something, even if they're not feeling the love.

Those first four needs are human or primal needs. No matter what, we will find ways to fulfill those on a daily basis, if even in very insignificant ways. Now, compare the first four needs to these last two needs, which are our spiritual needs as human beings.

5) Growth: We all have a need to grow. If we're not growing, improving, leveling up, then we often feel like we're dying, shrinking, or wasting our time. If a relationship isn't growing, if you're not learning new things, or if you're not moving your way up the corporate ladder, these are all examples of things we must feel; otherwise, we'll feel like we're not truly living. Men will often begin to question even their existence, if they're not engaged with something that fulfills their need for continued growth.

6) Contribution: We all have a desire to contribute to something greater than ourselves. It's in our human nature to be a part of the collective and to support it in the continual progress of humanity. This is often where a man will feel led to fulfill his purpose as a King, to contribute to a lasting legacy, and to shift his focus from a life of acquisition to a life of impact.

The cool thing is that how we differ as human beings is determined by how we prioritize these six needs and, more specifically, how we ultimately value two of these needs more than the other four.

Are you primarily motivated by love and contribution?

Or are you driven more by certainty and significance?

The biggest "ah-ha" I had, when Tony Robbins first asked me to put these six needs in priority order, from most to least valued? That my initial answer was *not,* in fact, how I spent my time.

For instance, I'd always thought nothing was more important than love and uncertainty, aka variety, adventure, spontaneity. Primarily, because of my childhood wound of not having the relationship with my parents I'd always wanted, I had always viewed myself as a hopeless romantic, and I loved the idea of giving my future children the childhood I wished I had been given.

And yet, when Robbins had each of us take an even closer look at how we lived our lives, especially when we felt stressed, what I discovered was I was spending most of my time working or traveling for my job, because my drive was to create "certainty" in the form of financial stability.

The close second to "certainty" was my drive for "significance." Reason being, I was desperate for validation, due to my low self-esteem at the time.

So, even though I initially thought I was driven by my needs of romantic love and a desire to experience life as an adventure, the harsh reality was very different. As it turned out, I was actually more concerned with making money, so I could provide a quality life, something I felt was my responsibility to do for my family at the time.

I used the fact that I was the primary breadwinner of our family as a way to feel significant, and to make myself feel good, because I believed I was supporting my spouse by following *her* dreams.

Martyring myself to a job I was passionless about (and at which I made good money) was my unhealthy way to feel significant. And since I was really insecure at the time, it was an easy way for me to meet my needs. At least, until I was awoken by the Tony Robbins event in 2009.

I realized on the first day of the seminar that I was driven to seek out situations where I had control, where I felt important, unique, and special. Not surprisingly, Robbins explained that the two needs valued most by ninety percent of people on the planet are...

1. Being Significant

We live in a social-media world. We often present a highlight reel of only our good times. This incomplete reality, rather than bring us closer together, often separates us.

These days, how often do we see people on social media put their own physical wellbeing in harm's way, only to create a video that goes viral?

2. Certainty

People want to be certain before they can do something. We all want to be guaranteed a positive outcome before we take the necessary risks. But that's not realistic. For instance, how could you ever start a business, if you had to be certain it would succeed before you started it?

Could you ever build a great relationship as long as your motivation was based on certainty? If you did, then everybody would have to stay the same and never change. All that means is you'd never grow, which in turn means you're going to be miserable.

Do you think you'd be successful at changing your health, if you first had to be sure you would never fall off the wagon or have a few slip ups?

Of course not.

In fact, growth is stimulated by uncertainty. And the quality of your life is affected by the amount of uncertainty you can reasonably manage, day-to-day.

What I learned from Tony Robbins's seminars and teachings was this: the key to living a life of absolute fulfillment is valuing *Growth* and *Contribution* above all else.

This is not something you can fake. You must be at a place where your true intention for growing and giving back to a greater good are congruent with your life's purpose and calling.

If it's not? If you live from a place of desiring certainty and significance, like the way I lived most of my life? The cost can be extremely destructive to you and others.

For example: my greatest need growing up was to be certain that people liked me. On that side of the coin, I also deeply needed to feel worthy; to feel special, unique, and significant. All of this led me to being a passive "nice guy." Which almost killed me.

It was like a self-sabotaging cocktail. I wanted everyone to like me. However, I also wanted to be crazy and fun, so people would notice me. As a result, in the process of being someone who was addicted to shock humor and entertainment, I naturally pissed people off. And sometimes they wouldn't like me.

Then I would go out of my way to get them to like me again, being an overly nice, passive ass-kisser. When my efforts weren't rewarded, I'd hate myself for being so "weak."

It was this vicious circle. One where I'd bounce between being a really "nice guy" and being a passive-aggressive prick.

On my podcast, I got to interview Dr. Robert Glover. He wrote a book in 2003 that had a huge impact on me, called, *No More Mr. Nice Guy: A Proven Plan for Getting What You Want in Love, Sex, and Life.*

Toward the beginning of the book, he offers the history and origin of the "nice guy." The book goes on to explain that, prior to the Industrial Revolution, young boys learned how to become men by spending time at their father's side, working the land, doing what men did. Likewise, little girls learned how to become women by spending time with their mothers and the other women of the homestead.

However, with the innovation of machines and the arrival of the Industrial Revolution, the work that had been traditionally the responsibility of men was relinquished. Far fewer men and women were required to work the land, as machines began to replace them.

As a result, men were forced to find other ways to provide for their families. And thus, they were often forced away from the home, to seek work in cities. With this shift came the birth of the "nice guy."

Boys were left at home to be raised by their moms, their sisters, aunts, school teachers—essentially, the women of the village. Through no fault of their own, the women were put into the position of doing the very best they could to raise well-mannered, good-natured boys.

The issue, however, is a woman cannot teach a boy how to be a man. Just as a man cannot teach a little girl how to be a woman. And this has been the case historically with boys being raised by the women of their family, while their absent fathers work and sacrifice quality time at home in the hopes they can somehow provide their families better lives than what they experienced, growing up.

So, year after year, generation after generation, boys were taught to be nice. To be good little boys, to mind their manners, and to restrain themselves. This has resulted in a gender confusion unlike any we've seen in history.

Speaking solely for myself, I grew up emulating the warriors and heroes I saw in my cartoons and in movies. I was a child of the eighties and came of age in the nineties. So, I emulated the examples of G.I. Joe, Voltron, He-Man, the Dukes of Hazzard, Knight Rider, the Flash, Conan the Barbarian, Rambo, William Wallace, Maximus Aurelius, and King Leonidas.

Many of these fictional characters, with their hyper-alpha masculinity, filled a void left empty by the lack of true and congruent masculine examples in my life.

Meanwhile, I was being taught by my mother to be a really nice boy and, eventually, a good man. A religious man who didn't swear, didn't smoke, didn't drink, and didn't have sex before he was married.

There were times I got in trouble. But when my mom caught wind of something bad I had done, my older brother recalls hearing her say, "No, not my sweet angel, Johnny?"

That's what I was to my mom: a sweet, innocent angel.

Even so, what I truly longed for was an adventure to live. What I didn't realize at the time is that the masculine heart desires to be tested. The masculine heart responds to challenge and finds its self-worth through overcoming those challenges. This is why I devoured stories of World War II and of the ancient Roman conquests. I desperately desired a battle to fight. And I wondered if I'd ever truly be called upon to be in one.

Rewind the Clock

Early in 2020 during the very beginning of the coronavirus pandemic, I spent time babysitting my girlfriend's five-year-old boy while she worked and his school was closed.

It was fascinating to watch this little five-year-old spend hours playing by himself, with nothing more than his imagination, just as I remember doing when I was his age.

He was constantly making loud noises. Things blowing up, crashes of Matchbox cars, epic LEGO battles between opposing forces—it seemed as though bloodshed was required for this little guy to have fun.

"I just don't get it," his mother would tell me. "Where does all this aggression come from?"

I replied with a tear of pride in my eye, "It comes from within. He's a masculine boy. And love it or hate it, he needs to attack something, hit something, blow something up. It's just what the masculine soul does to express itself sometimes."

To sit down with stuffed animals and pretend to have tea doesn't make sense to masculine-wired boys, who are always on a quest to become a hero.

The masculine heart is always looking for a focal point, something to aim at. Whereas the feminine heart is often looking at how it can connect and inherently understands that the point of sitting down to tea is to share an experience together.

This provoked a powerful series of conversations between me and my friend about her son. We discussed the differences in behavior between people who are more masculine-wired vs. those who are more feminine-wired, so we could better understand each other, and why we do what we do as men and women.

Masculine vs. Feminine

If the concepts of "masculine" and "feminine" are new to you, let me explain.

People understandably confuse "masculine" with "male" and "feminine" with "female." However, the truth is we all—men and women—express a wide array of both masculine and feminine qualities.

Most (but not all) people will have an orientation as to whether they feel more at home when they're in their masculine or feminine energy. I like to refer to this as someone's hard-wiring.

For instance, I'm hard-wired masculine. It's where I prefer to be, and it's what my brain defaults to. When talking to people, I naturally ask the question in my mind, *What's your motivation in telling me this? How can I help?* My natural instinct is to look for any solution I can offer.

To give some more insight, the masculine mind is often looking for what the point is, trying to determine where things are headed, in order to minimize anything that may impede its progress toward attaining the ultimate goal.

On the other hand, the feminine mind often looks to connect, to fill up. It seeks out the validation of that connection in order to express itself. It's focused on the present moment and on enjoying the journey happening right here and now.

What I have come to realize (something I'd lost from my younger years) was I still had in me the same fierceness I recognized in that five-year-old's heart. Over years of learning to value myself by gaining the approval of my mom, my sister, and all the other women who had been given the task of keeping me in line, however, I eventually learned to become that sweet little angel my mom always wanted me to be.

Essentially, I was trained to shut down my masculine wiring and embrace the more feminine parts of me. Without the balance of a healthy expression of both the masculine and feminine, I became one-dimensional.

I became boring.

I was neither wild, dangerous nor free.

Prior to my wake-up call at age thirty, I was stuck in a cubicle, working a job I was passionless about. I would come home as a boring, predictable, and emotionally flatlined shell of a man. And you know what? There was nothing attractive about that man.

My life imploding was the greatest gift I've ever received. It reawakened the part inside my heart that had fallen dormant. It reawakened the sense of adventure I had forgotten was written upon my heart. It reawakened the masculine man who had succumbed to mediocrity.

My mom's passing, my dad coming out of the closet, and my divorce—all of this culminated in a calling for me to shed the exoskeleton of the "nice guy" and step into a brand-new adventure.

An adventure—and life—I could fall in love with!

I undertook a path of discovery into my heart to see if, in fact, I had what it took to be a man of purpose.

And, my brother, I believe *you* have the same wiring I do. I believe, if you've been living a life that's below what you're capable of experiencing, you are robbing yourself—and all those who love you—of seeing the man you were meant to become.

Namely: a man who is balanced in expressing his masculine and feminine character traits.

All of this may sound like a pipe dream. You may doubt you have what it takes to become that man, a man you can be truly proud of. But listen, brother: I, too, had *massive* doubts as I began the journey to improve.

I would often say I was happy with the life I was living, before the shit hit the fan. But I was lying. The reality was I was scared, playing small, playing it safe, and willing to accept "good enough."

Scared of not knowing what would be required of me to evolve. Scared of stepping up to a lot of my discomfort on my quest to heal.

I feared finding out that I didn't have what it took to be the man I always wanted to be. So, out of that fear, I convinced myself it was safer not to go for it. I convinced myself that a "safe" life was better than a life of not measuring up and not being loved.

Is this resonating?

If it is, then the time has come for you, as it did for me, to be done with a life that is safe and boring.

It is time you cross the threshold and become the man who has it all. The man who follows through on his heart's desire.

The man who can be trusted, is respected, and whose word is his bond.

This is a man who lives his life authentically and with integrity. And I'm here to tell you: *you can become that man.*

CHAPTER 6

Achievement & Fulfillment

"Happiness is a state of inner fulfillment, not the gratification of inexhaustible desires for outward things."

—Matthieu Ricard

Dial #2: An Extraordinary Life on Your Terms

MANY PEOPLE CONFUSE being *rich* with being *wealthy*.

In his books, *The Millionaire Next Door* and *Stop Acting Rich*, Joseph Stanley explains how the rich—those who often seek the limelight—are those who spend their money on the acquisition of material things. And yet, they are often still addicted, lost, and unfulfilled.

Compare that to those who are truly wealthy; those who may or may not have acquired just as much and yet are deeply fulfilled. And why is that?

To piggyback upon what Stanley says: while the rich spend their money on things that fulfill their needs for significance and to look successful, tangible goods can never fill the deep void of a lack of self-worth.

In his book, Stanley goes on to say that the truly wealthy spend their money on experiences, things that create memories. They also spend a lot of their time and money on growth and education. So, they're constantly investing back into themselves and their loved ones.

Why do I tell you this? It's because—as I mentioned at the conclusion of explaining the six human needs—to be truly fulfilled, you must set your life up in a way that your two primary needs are *Growth* and *Contribution*. You must develop a commitment to constantly learn and expand who you are while also contributing to something far greater than yourself.

If you want to live a life of purpose, you must find reasons that compel you that far exceed your own personal needs and desires. Now, let's take a look at some of the ways we can achieve that.

As Tony Robbins says, "Success without fulfillment is the ultimate failure."

Mastering the skill of the *Science of Achievement* means to take what you envision and make it a reality. This is often what business looks like. How can you make something quicker, faster, cheaper, better, and/or easier? How can you improve profit margins? How can you sell more units?

As humans, we often put on a pedestal those individuals who have the ability to manifest what they envision and make it real. We're often asking ourselves, "How did they create those results?" It's a skillset you can learn, often by modeling what works, discovering the shortcuts, and acquiring the strategies.

Why it's a "science" is simple. Take earning money as an example. Anyone can learn how to make money with the right mentorship and teaching. However, I can also tell you, while there are a lot of people who have mastered making money, many still don't live extraordinary lives. They're still miserable, lonely, addicted to drugs, sex, drinking, work. No matter how much money they make, it's never enough.

It may look like an extraordinary life because *you* see it as extraordinary, compared to how you live yours. However, behind the scenes of the social media world and the realm of business, there are multi-millionaires and billionaires who are flat-out *miserable* as hell.

So, what's the secret to achieving our wildest dreams *and* being happy? It's the other side of the coin: the Art of Fulfillment.

If you want an extraordinary life, you can't just achieve. You must also seek fulfillment. As simplistic as that sounds, it's true.

What fulfillment looks like to each of us is different; there are as many differing versions of fulfillment as there are people on the planet. Because of this, most people will see someone with the results they want and think, *Yeah, I want to get that*. They will model everything they do on someone else's success, and it might even work at first. They may achieve the very things they wanted to achieve. And yet, they may still be surprised when it doesn't fulfill them like they thought it would.

How many people do you know who chased their dreams, got what they thought they wanted, and still weren't fulfilled? "Is this all there is?" they ask.

Over the years, I've had a lot of conversations with men who, intellectually, get everything I just explained. However, they remain paralyzed around "finding" their purpose. They think, if they can just "find" their purpose, their passion in life, *then* they will be fulfilled and happy.

However, as they come up with ideas, they constantly compare themselves to others and ask, "Is my purpose big enough? Is it strong enough? Is it clear enough?"

I'm reminded of the classic quote that comes to us courtesy of President Theodore Roosevelt: "Comparison is the thief of joy."

Don't waste your time seeking your elusive purpose. Rather, do what's right in front of you and give it hell.

In a podcast interview with one of my amazing coaches, thought leader and philosopher Rob Scott, he recommends you, "Choose your purpose, don't wait to 'find' it."

Give it all you've got. Focus on giving and not on receiving, and you'll end up receiving more than you could ever imagine!

The person who is always attempting to "get"? No one wants to deal with that person. They're takers.

The secret to living is giving. It's whatever makes *you* feel alive, because you're no longer in scarcity.

And how do you get out of scarcity? It's a habit. It's as simple as finding someone and genuinely complimenting them without any ulterior motive. Or helping someone who is in need and in a difficult situation.

You see, I refer to it as an art because art is in the eye of the beholder. It's subjective. What I might find attractive or cool may be the worst thing you've ever seen or heard.

So, to take your art of fulfillment—what truly makes you happy—and compare it to someone else's art? That is a complete waste of time. No one is going to tell you what makes you happy and fulfilled. How could they? The answer to what makes you content is already within you. To access it, all you must do is ask.

Am I saying that the key to happiness is to seek only your art and, thus, starve? Hell no. Remember: they're two sides of the same coin. You must have both to be truly happy. There are a lot of starving artists out there who love their craft but who also worry if they're going to make rent next month.

Instead, I want you to focus on abundance. A King is someone who exemplifies both achievement *and* fulfillment. A man who has mastered both science and art. This is at the core of every man who yearns to join his brothers in Becoming Kings.

CHAPTER 7

The Fork

"Success in life is the result of good judgment. Good judgment is usually the result of experience. Experience is usually the result of bad judgment."
—Tony Robbins

Dial #3: Decisions

REMEMBER: WHAT YOU FOCUS on is what you feel. And to change your focus, your fastest option is to move your body and decide how to use your physiology.

The next fastest way to change your focus is by the power of questions. Meaning, we all have patterns to the questions we ask ourselves, which ultimately direct where our thoughts go and the meaning we assign to life's events.

This is precisely where your emotional fitness comes into play. Because, as soon as you experience something, your brain goes right to asking itself, *What does this mean?* If you're not fit and resilient, you'll allow your brain to assign meaning passively. This will then instantly produce emotions within you that will affect your actions, and your actions will go on to shape the results you get in life.

The real problem is—most likely—you have been conditioned to let the world and the environment train you to think like everybody else. You're emotionally unfit.

So how do you get emotionally fit, you ask?

Are most men healthy, vibrant, strong, and vital? Are most men in a passionate relationship for decades; one where they don't just hang out, but they truly love their partner? Do most men have a career, job, or business that they love and cannot wait to get out of bed to go to every day? Are most men in integrity with their word, where, if they say to someone (or to themselves) they're going to do something, they follow through? For most men, the answer is no. But there are a few that do.

And why is this?

It's because most men are only focused on the *Science of Achievement*. At the end of the day, they're dying for a life of meaning. A life of meaning they're hoping someone other than them can provide the answers to.

See, the key to living the life of a King—a life of true fulfillment, where you have it all—is to choose something or someone you care for so much, you'll do anything for them. It's only then that the greatest part of you will appear.

When you get clear on the mission that you're on for yourself, your lover, your family, your brothers, your community, and the world, then *you're not going to suffer anymore.*

In life, you're either going to suffer or grow. If you're suffering, you haven't grown yet. If you're suffering, you're making it all about you. Suffering will continue and growth will not occur until a new set of beliefs takes you beyond your limited focus of what is possible.

The truth is, brother, a worthy opponent is what creates a great hero. You have a great story to write in the living of your life. However, nothing will change until you do. Nothing will change until you harness the power of making a clear decision to raise your standards.

Once we make that decision, everything can change. The decisions we make control so much more than the conditions we find ourselves in. Because it's not the conditions that have power. It's our decisions that do.

It's your decisions on what to *believe*, your decisions on what to *do*, and your decisions on what to *give* during this one life that creates a life of meaning.

When I think back fifteen, ten, even five years ago about the decisions I've made, I see the direct impact they've had on the quality of my life and the fulfillment I now enjoy. And I bet it's the same for you. For better or for worse, I bet your life is completely different now than it was back then, based on a few key decisions.

The *most important decision* you could ever make—above any on the face of the Earth—is to decide, no matter what happens in your life, you're going to choose and commit to living in an empowering emotional state.

Your decision must be this: regardless of whether pain arises, you choose not to suffer. To reiterate, suffering is when you make it about you while you get angry or get worried or frustrated—anything that takes your attention away from living from an abundance mindset.

From an abundance mindset, you no longer focus on yourself. Rather, you focus on something *greater* than yourself.

What a lot of men don't realize is our brains were never designed to make us happy. Our brain's primary function is to constantly scan situations and environments in order to protect us and survive. It is always looking for what could be a threat; what could be wrong. And because of this two-million-year-old design, it's very natural for a part of you to be okay with safety. The status quo. Okay with being ordinary, mediocre, and living a life that is "good enough."

Only you can build a firm foundation of life off your successes. Rather than look constantly at what you could be doing to be more successful, more productive, to be healthier, I want you to decide to end the suffering. I want you to learn that suffering is all about the ego; it's you obsessing about you. And don't go confusing suffering with pain. Pain, resistance, and discomfort are the price of admission to having a fulfilled life.

Suffering is based within a foundation of fear. And the antidote to fear is gratitude. I want you to attempt to be simultaneously fearful and grateful. It's not actually possible. You cannot genuinely be grateful while also being fearful at the same time. That's why gratitude is the bedrock to you remaining in control of your emotional state.

Let's get real for a minute, though. You're not going to get out of this human experience without going through some tragedy and heartache. Like me, you may lose a family member. And if you haven't, you will. You may get a divorce. Your business may fail. There may be another global pandemic. The government may shut down your business. You might go bankrupt.

I hope, for your sake, you won't have to go through most of these examples. And I'm not saying you necessarily will. However, there's no way to predict what's really going to happen in your life. Life's full of uncertainty.

Here's what you *can* know: you have the freedom to decide, no matter what happens to you, you're going to look for the opportunity to thrive.

Have you ever read the book, *Man's Search for Meaning*, by Viktor Frankl? This book is by far one of my favorites. It's about Frankl's personal story of being locked up in Auschwitz and finding *joy* in the middle of a Jewish concentration camp during World War II.

To think that your outside circumstances determine how you feel is to massively undersell yourself on what you're capable of.

If you fall into the trap of believing **your** way of behaving in life is the *only* way people must behave, then you're always going to be unhappy.

If you believe your spouse, significant other, your kids, your parents, your siblings, your boss, and/or your co-workers all have to behave a specific way for you to experience peace when you're around them, then you're attempting to paddle upstream without an oar.

My great invitation to you is this: realize that as wonderful as it is to provide, to protect, and to achieve, it's just as important to enjoy this life. Without enjoyment, you'll never become the King of your kingdoms.

American speaker and author Byron Katie has what she refers to as "The Work." (Katie, Byron. *Loving What Is: Four Questions That Can Change Your Life*. New York, New York: Harmony Books, 2002.) It's a method for creating greater awareness around the emotions and meanings we generate that often disempower us.

What she recommends is to notice someone or something that pisses you off, and then write down why you're pissed about that specific situation.

While you're thinking and writing about that specific situation, allow yourself to get petty, childish, judgmental, and free of censorship. Really. It's important.

Once you have the scenario captured on paper, she asks you to isolate one thought or inquiry, and then ask yourself the following questions, specifically in this order:

1. Is it true?
2. Can you absolutely know it's true?
3. How do you react, what happens, when you believe that thought?
4. Who would you be without that thought?

Lastly, she recommends you then turn the thought around by asking, "Is the opposite true or truer than the original thought?"

Trust me, there may be a part of you that thinks this is crazy. I promise you, though: it works incredibly well. And in doing it, it allows you to take full responsibility for any situation or thought.

To take responsibility for your emotional fitness—to understand where you're committed to feeling passionate, playful, curious, loving, or excited—you will treat others a thousand times better than when you're feeling lonely, worried, pissed, depressed, overwhelmed, and/or being a victim to life.

Truth is, you get to decide if life happens to you, or *for you*!

Brother, you know as well as I do that coming from that place of abundance, you're going to be a better lover, a better parent, and a better person. People will want to do business with you, to be around you. And overall, your life is going to be a thousand times more enjoyable!

So, this is my point: the most important power you wield as a man and human being is your ability to *decide*. Decide today you're no longer willing to settle. Instead, decide you're going to live in an abundant mindset. Just to be clear, you will have your ups and downs. You will have your shitty days where things get out of hand. Still, with the power to decide, you can choose not to stay in that unhealthy mindset.

Decide to let go of the resistance to how you expect life should go, and exchange it for gratitude. When you do this, your experience of life will change dramatically. If you're able to appreciate the little things in life, the unexpected moments of beauty, the look in your lover's eyes, the smell of flowers in the air during an early morning run—then you truly are becoming a King.

If you are not able to appreciate the little moments, then I'll tell you right now, more muscle, less fat, more money, more passion, more vacation, more business, more of anything will still not ever bring you more happiness and fulfillment.

As the saying goes, if you're not able to save ten cents out of a dollar now, what makes you think you'll be able to save a hundred thousand out of a million? If you're not willing to do it in the here and now, then chances are you aren't going to do it when you have more.

Being *rich* is about the acquisition of more "things," while being *wealthy* is about having appreciation for everything you have in the moment. People are often in the pursuit of becoming rich in the future. The reality is, you can be wealthy in this moment when you look at everything you are blessed with in your life.

Crossing the Threshold

Speaking of the power of making decisions, you are now at a crossroads. The proverbial fork in the road.

I've told a lot of my story up to this point. My hope is there's been a lot you've been able to relate to or see yourself in. Yes, my circumstances and details differ from that of your own story. However, there comes a time when you must make a decision and cross the threshold.

You have to make the decision to say, "I've had enough of my mediocre life. It must improve now!"

This decision for you, in your life, signifies your commitment to your journey to do whatever it takes to become your best version every fucking day.

I don't believe you pick up a book like this and begin turning its pages unless you truly desire to become extraordinary. You don't pick up a book like this unless there's at least a small part of you that believes you're a leader.

The reality is, whether you choose to remain in mediocrity or to level-up, both options are challenging. Remaining ordinary and accepting "good enough" in life often results in suffering. Leveling-up however, while also challenging, is greatly motivating.

It's just like being in the gym: when you push yourself to failure, that's when muscles grow the most. Life is no different. You will continue to have those challenges on the path of becoming a man you can be proud of.

One of the biggest challenges I have worked to overcome is allowing myself to be emasculated, to play small, to not express my true masculine core. As I mentioned previously, my father was a workaholic as I was growing up, so I rarely saw him, and even when he was around, he wasn't emotionally present. I only know this because I have very few memories of him from my childhood.

Given his absence, I was primarily raised by women. I had a lot of opportunity to nurture and develop my feminine attributes, which I am deeply appreciative of now, as an adult.

The development of my masculine has not been easy. However, it comes a lot more naturally than being sensitive, emotional, and empathetic, which I learned from the feminine-wired women in my life.

One thing I've learned the hard way is how my past patterns of behavior deeply impacted my ability to truly be present. Let me explain...

When I was growing up, my father was absent so much that my mother naturally got her needs for love met by myself and my four other siblings. Not surprisingly, I became a "momma's boy."

My older brother filled in as best he could in the role of a father. Even so, at just four years older than I, he was busy learning from trial-and-error, as well.

I learned from an early age, when my mother needed support, love, and to be seen, I was able to comfort and validate her.

I remember her asking my siblings and me if she was a good mother. What I didn't realize as a child was how detrimental this behavior would be to me.

By relying on her children to give her the love and validation she actually needed from her husband (a.k.a. my father), she unrealistically placed a level of responsibility on us that was unfair for any of us to bear.

Did she do it intentionally? Absolutely not. However, that doesn't negate the fact that it had an immense impact on me in later years.

For instance, when it was time for me to go off to college, there was a part of me that took into consideration my mother's feelings when I considered attending schools that were far from home. At the end of the day, I chose a college that was only an hour away from where I grew up, because I knew how much it would mean to her to have me close. This is a great example of "co-dependency."

She took full advantage, too. She rarely missed a single sporting event of mine or my siblings for as long as I can remember.

In retrospect, I now realize, as a masculine-wired man, pulling away and creating space from loved ones is what is required of me to reenergize. However, because of my mother's needs, I suppressed a ton of my own masculine needs and surrendered my responsibility to take care of myself.

Instead, I became that really sweet young man. The "nice guy" she had raised me to be. One who was very thoughtful, sensitive, pleasing, passive, codependent, and enmeshed.

I didn't realize until later that, while I gained feeling significant and loved by my mom, I ended up losing touch with huge parts of myself, including my masculine power, my desires, my passions, my freedoms. When I think back on it, I was afraid. I was afraid to speak up for what I needed.

The more I went on like this, the more the anger and resentment built up within me. This required so much energy to repress that I would eventually fall into ruts of apathy and numbness.

In my relationships in high school, college, and when I was married, I often felt ashamed and confused. Because whomever I was in relationship with would feed my sense of self-worth. And yet, I simultaneously felt a natural pull to create distance.

Distance was a thing I wasn't giving myself. I had this romantic sense of love. And just as I had always made myself available to my mother whenever she needed me, my future relationships with women weren't much different. I was afraid, if I spoke up for my need to create space, or to speak *any* of my needs, my partner would stop loving me.

In being so close to my mother, I inherently felt the pain she experienced of not having my father around. So, I really struggled to find balance between being close and honoring my need for autonomy and independence.

After years of being a "momma's boy" and realizing that "nice guys" do in fact finish last, I began to feel resentful. Welling up inside me was a rebel, a man who was sick and tired of doing all the right things. At the age of thirty, when my life imploded, I began to rebel against everything I had known. Deep below the surface, a resentment, anger, and rage had been building.

What I have come to learn from various coaches is that it is completely natural for a man to blow off steam, to find healthy ways to release his pent-up anger, and to create space to reenergize.

Man's Natural Needs

Just as women have a monthly menstrual cycle, we, too, as men, have a natural intimacy cycle.

Men experience being close and connected. However, after a period of intimacy, they need to pull away and do something masculine. Have you ever experienced this?

Countless men have explained to me that they can spend time watching a "romantic comedy," being affectionate with their significant other, and having deep and meaningful conversation. However, they eventually feel the pull to turn on something that involves fighting or things blowing up, to fix something around the house, or to get things done in order to feel rebalanced. Not all men will experience this, but for those who are hardwired masculine, this is normal.

If they've spent time being present with their significant other, expressing their feelings and being vulnerable, they'll eventually feel this inner drive to create space, to go for a run, or to get back to "doing"—checking things off their to-do list. Masculine men are hardwired to produce and provide results. It is the hunter/gatherers within us.

"I could only lie on the couch and 'cuddle' for so long before I had to get up and get stuff done!" one man told me.

Now, if for any reason this *doesn't* resonate with you at all, then you may be on the other side of the spectrum.

And that's fine! Some men have no issue with pulling away. In fact, they're *really* good at it. So good at it, the challenge for this type of man is they struggle to come back at all. Opening up, vulnerability, and intimacy are extremely difficult for men of this type.

They won't admit it openly, but they're scared of the intimacy, of caring for someone. They may even feel they're unworthy of love. They have no idea how that would even look or how welcomed they'd be, if they allowed themselves to get close.

The problem arises when either man doesn't honor what he needs. If the "nice guy" suppresses this need for space, he'll often begin feeling resentful and smothered. The man who is avoidant and so good at creating space that he has a hard time voicing his wants and needs can come up with a story that he's unlovable.

So, whether you feel you're more sensitive or you're afraid to feel anything at all, men on both sides of the spectrum, and anywhere in between, can have difficulty realizing they, too, have this natural intimacy pattern. Without understanding and recognizing you have this pattern of pulling away—and then springing back to be close—your intimate relationships will be severely impacted.

These are all things I've unfortunately learned the hard way. And this is exactly why I've written this book. I've done it in the hopes it'll help you navigate the things many of us do unknowingly; things that could save you a ton of pain, if you know what to look for!

If you want to learn more about this cycle of needing closeness and then space, read *Men are from Mars, Women are from Venus: The Classic Guide to Understanding the Opposite Sex* by John Gray, as well as the book, *Attached: The New Science of Adult Attachment and How it Can Help You Find – and Keep – Love* by Amir Levine and Rachel Heller.

CHAPTER 8

Your Blueprint for Life

"It is never too late to be who you might have been."

—George Elliot

EARLIER IN THIS BOOK, we discussed that what controls our lives is the emotional states we live in. If you're *pissed,* you're going to treat people completely different than if you're *excited.*

To review, pleasure is always something you obtain from outside sources. It just never lasts long. It's like getting a brand-new phone or gadget. How long is it until it feels like just another device? A couple of days, max.

Compare that to happiness, which is achieved by looking within. And unlike pleasure, it lasts. The hard part is that pleasure comes in the form of instant gratification and can be found everywhere, whereas happiness often feels more elusive, even though the ability to tap into it within ourselves is always present. Not surprisingly, to live a life of absolute abundance, seeking happiness is where it's at.

Now, it's crucial to be aware that, although happiness is what you're after, it's extremely easy to fall into a rut of being addicted to pleasure. When we get stressed, pleasure is a lot easier to use as a way to alleviate pain, in the short term. That's why I spoke about the building blocks of emotions, and how you must take control of using your physiology (your body) in a healthy way.

By putting your body to good use, it'll help you to control what you focus on. When you're feeling good and healthy by taking care of your body, even the language you use to describe what you're focusing on creates healthier meanings around what you experience in life.

Remember, *the quality of your life is directly proportional to the quality of the questions you ask yourself.* Said another way, what you focus on is what you feel; what determines your focus is the questions you're asking. I know I've said this several times already, however it's on purpose. We learn from what we repeatedly hear, say, or do.

The challenge is this: what often stop you from moving forward are limiting beliefs and the fear that you're not enough. That you won't be loved. Your fears are magnified by how they're triggered; by a set of belief systems, your sense of identity, and your values and rules. It's the good and bad experiences of your life that tint the lens through which you view life.

I like to think of it as your blueprint for life. It consists of five areas that affect how you see your life:

1. Universal Beliefs: What are your beliefs about the purposes of life and death? What do you believe causes pain, and what creates happiness? We all have beliefs about time, people, love, money, work, relationships, emotions, etc., that play into how we view our day-to-day lives.

For instance, before I sat down to intentionally rewrite the blueprint for how I envisioned my life, it had been unintentionally established by all the things I had experienced in my life up till that point. What is pain? What is pleasure? What is success? How should life be lived?

2. Identity: Your identity has everything to do with how you envision yourself. Who are you? Who are you *not*? What is your

life about? What's the story of your life? How would you describe your archetypes, stage of life, quality of life?

Before my thirties, I believed the purpose of life was to be a "nice guy," to have everyone like me, and to ensure everyone was happy. I tried to accomplish this by going out of my way to be thoughtful, considerate, and proactive in providing for people's needs, even before they needed something.

For a long time, it was like I had a clearer vision of who I *didn't* want to be in life than who I did want to be.

I've had countless conversations with men and women over the years who, in reply to my question, "What are you looking for in a significant other?" say, "Well I know what I *don't* want! Let me tell you..."

The truth is, your brain is like a laser-guided missile. The RAS or Reticular Activating System is the area of the brain responsible for how you perceive the world. The interesting thing about it is that it doesn't know the difference between reality when you're awake or when you're asleep. That's why, when you're dreaming, you don't know it. Whatever you give your RAS to focus on, either what you want or don't want, it will hit the target. The key is this: the target itself is up to you to determine.

3. Fundamental Question: What do you primarily focus on day-to-day versus for your life? What question do you ask most often?

I've learned from attending Tony Robbin's *Date with Destiny* event that we all have a fundamental question that influences and guides our focus on a moment-to-moment basis. For instance, some people's questions are...

- How can I win?
- Why aren't I ever good enough?
- How can I make this better?

- What's the point?
- Am I lovable?
- What's wrong with me?

The list goes on and on. For me, the fundamental question I was constantly asking was, "Am I truly special?"

I had always felt this desire to become a leader, someone who made a positive impact on others, and yet I also always struggled with a lack of self-confidence. What I didn't consciously understand was that this fundamental question was constantly creating a huge sense of self-doubt and insecurity within me. It supported a limiting belief that I was a waste of potential. When I made a mistake, it would support my limiting belief, as I'd often think to myself, *See, you're clearly not special.*

So, when you learn what your fundamental question is, it can open your world up to a ton of clarity as to why you are the way you are.

The beautiful thing is you can actually choose to write a new empowering question to guide your life forward from here on, if you're willing to do the work. If you are, I cannot recommend more highly that you take any of Tony Robbins's events and workshops, as they've been absolute game changers in my life.

4. Values: Desires & Fears. Why is it that we often know what we *should* do, and yet we don't bring ourselves to doing it? If you've ever felt like you've sabotaged something good in your life, it's because of a conflict in values.

There will often be direct conflicts between what we desire and what we fear. For instance, let's say you really want to lose weight, which requires you to be on a diet. However, your biggest fear is being alone, cut off from your loved ones. Thus, when it comes to the decision of going out to dinner with friends or choosing to remain on a diet, if one of your worst fears is to feel cut off from those you love most or left behind, chances are good you'll choose to eat what everyone else is eating, instead of stick to your diet. This all makes more sense when you're reminded that we'll always do more to avoid pain than we will do to gain pleasure.

Missing out on connecting with friends and eating delicious food would be way more painful than extending being on a diet a couple more days. At least, that's how most people weigh out their options.

5. Rules: Your set of beliefs in the form of rules that support maintaining or growing your identity. Whether you like it or not, you have rules that you believe people should conform to, and if they don't, you get upset.

Example: People should always remain completely quiet while watching a movie at the theatre.

Example: If someone really appreciates me, they'll remember my birthday and will reach out to wish me a happy birthday.

Example: When someone loves me, they should show it by doing things for me.

We all have countless rules, and because of their subtleness, we tend to fail to recognize them. That is, unless you begin asking yourself probing questions to bring them to the surface. Such as...

How do you like to feel loved or appreciated?

What needs to happen so you feel loved, appreciated, and respected?

What has to happen for you to feel seen and validated for doing good work at your job?

The answers to these questions begin to offer insight into your rules as to how you judge whether you're winning or losing at life.

Life Tests

In life, you're going to be constantly tested. During the journey of overcoming those tests, you will have allies and enemies who will play important roles in your growth as a man. More times than not, the enemies who wage war against you will come from within. Your world beliefs, your identity, or sense of self, your fundamental question, your values, and your rules will all play a massive role in creating your blueprint of the world.

As an example, prior to opening my first gym in late 2010 and after quitting my corporate job, I had been unemployed for nearly four months and was working on my very first website. It was called Lose100PoundsForGood.com, and it sold a $47 digital product. Between a workbook and video modules, it supported unhealthy individuals by getting to the root of their emotional eating.

How big of a success was it?

I sold one unit. One order of $47.

At the time, I didn't believe in myself enough to think I was going to be successful with this offer. That said, what the project *did* provide me was a positive distraction from the otherwise depressing state of my life.

I was working on the website when an email dropped into my inbox. It was from my buddy, the entrepreneurial coach, Lewis Howes.

"Hey man," it said. "Check out this info product *How to Build a Six-Figure Bootcamp Business in 90 Days*. I think you could pull this off!"

Scratching my head, a lightbulb went off...

So many of the women I had been coaching said they wanted nothing to do with discussing the skeletons in their closets, particularly as they related to why they emotionally ate. What they wanted was help with losing weight. "Can you be my personal trainer?" they asked.

When Lewis sent me that email, what dawned on me was this was an answer. And a thought popped into my mind...

If I give them what they say they want (exercise and weight loss), they can be given what they truly need (mental and emotional transformation)!

The gym was a means to an end. Soon, I was off and running. I had the perfect location in mind for where I should open my first gym.

The following day, I walked in and struck a deal with the landlord. Within twenty-four hours, I signed a one-year lease for the space to conduct my St. Louis Fitness Bootcamp.

Walking out the doors that day with a signed lease in hand, the reality hit me. I had been living off credit cards the previous three months and was now on the hook for a monthly rent payment—all without having sold a single gym membership. I was simultaneously excited and scared out of my mind. *How was I going to pull this off?*

Well, what had worked in the previous months was something I learned from the Tony Robbins coach I'd hired. He had held me accountable to moving forward, little by little and day by day, in creating and producing my first website and digital product.

So, I thought to myself: *If it worked with that, why wouldn't I do that again?*

The first place I looked in order to hire a coach was with the creators of the $97 info product Lewis had sent me on how to start a six-figure bootcamp in ninety days. Sure enough, the creator (whose name was Steve) also did business coaching. So, I hired him. I whipped out that well-used credit card. Looking back at it now, it was a steal of a deal.

I hired Steve for a year of unlimited coaching for $3,000.

One of the first things he challenged me to do was to buy fifty lead boxes, and place them within a three-mile radius of my gym, to gather free leads.

If you aren't familiar with lead boxes, they're simply boxes with images on them of people working out. It promoted a raffle of a free month's gym membership people could win, if they just put their name and contact information on a piece of paper and slipped it into the box.

Next came the hard part: putting them out into the community. And I was scared as hell. To me, placing these things out there was just as bad as cold-calling strangers. The prospect of getting rejected was really difficult for me. And sure enough, I was up against massive resistance every day.

I'd wake up and dread walking out the door. I wanted to remain in bed. However, that rent was due soon! I struggled to psych myself up; to get the courage to walk into nail salons, hair salons, massage businesses, and anywhere else local midwestern women might frequent.

After two weeks into this experiment, I had only successfully placed seven of my fifty lead boxes. At that rate, I guesstimated it'd take months to place them all. And with each passing day, it seemed like the failure of my gym was becoming more and more imminent.

What also took the wind out of my sails was, when I went back every week to check on the seven lead boxes I'd placed, I'd walk away with maybe three total leads.

It was extremely disheartening.

With each month that I paid my monthly lease, I sank further into credit card debt and deeper into a well of sadness and fear.

And then one day, everything changed.

It was 10:30 on a Monday morning, and I had already been told "no" three times when I'd asked to place my lead boxes (for free, mind you) in someone's place of business. I sat in my car in silence, on the verge of tears, wondering what the hell I was going to do if this failed. In the back seat sat over forty lead boxes still waiting to find their homes.

All I wanted to do was go home and watch a movie or sleep or do *anything* to distract myself from the feeling that I was failing at life.

I just want to go home, I thought to myself. But then a different voice spoke up. *And do what? You have no couch, very little furniture, your apartment is only going to make you even more sad and lonely than you already are.*

Then I thought to myself, *If you go home, Johnny... nothing changes. You remain the same man who has gotten you into this mess. You'll remain the same man who also buried his head in the sand when you were married. If you want anything to change, you must continue to fail forward. What other options do you have? Really?*

Damn, I was getting the full court press put on by my inner coach. *By* me!

So, considering my options, I decided to continue doing just that: failing forward. And with that, I started my truck and drove a couple blocks to the next business on my list.

Before I could even finish my little sales pitch, the owner said, "Sure, go for it. Just leave it there on the counter."

"Really?"

Fast forward one hour from that defining moment in my truck, when I wanted to give up, and I had gotten three straight yeses. I was on cloud nine!

Talk about a day of riding an emotional roller coaster.

That morning I learned something extremely significant: if I don't give up—if I'm relentless—there's no way I'll fail.

In a recent podcast episode with the world-renowned MMA coach and owner of Factory X, Marc Montoya, he stated, "The failing part is the learning part."

Marc is the head coach for a large group of UFC fighters; I have seen their fight results on social media. Marc is a man of his word, and whether they win or lose, he's always beside them, coaching them into being greater athletes by learning from the moments when their opponents got the better of them.

He frequently reiterates that only through failing do we have the greatest opportunity for growth and learning.

That moment in my truck after a long morning of failing to place my lead boxes, feeling like all I wanted was to quit, and then I didn't—this was a massive turning point for me.

Now, let me be honest, it's not as if it was easy from there on. I struggled to keep putting one foot in front of the next. And with each subsequent "yes," the "noes" became less and less wounding. It was a *great* day when I finally placed that fiftieth lead box.

If my story had been a fairy tale, this is where I would go on to tell you how big a game-changer those lead boxes were on my business, right? Well, they weren't. They were a total flop.

With fifty lead boxes out in the community, I'd average five to ten leads every couple of weeks. It was pretty dismal, too, when I'd call on these leads, and people had no idea how I had gotten their info. Many of them hung up on me, chewed me out, and/or threatened to report me and my business to the BBB.

What I decided was, from my coach Steve's experience, people in California were a lot more willing to share their information than people in the Midwest.

So, with that realization firmly in hand, I had yet again another decision: give up and go home or pivot again. I chose the latter.

Not long after that, I was having coffee with a friend, and they told me about this new thing called Groupon. Another lightbulb went off.

Excited, I jumped online and applied... and immediately got denied. However, in my continued search, I stumbled upon a new competitor of Groupon, called LivingSocial.

I applied, and they accepted my offer. My business changed after that. It went from being on life support to thriving!

Within a week, my daily deal had run. And within the first twenty-four hours after it went live, ninety-one people had purchased a one-month package of unlimited bootcamp workouts.

I felt like I had hit the lottery. As far as I was concerned, I was *rich*! Ha-ha, not quite. Still, it wasn't even the money so much as it was the validation that people were looking for what I was offering. It was another huge lightbulb moment. I discovered, if you build it (and have proper marketing), people will come!

So, what happened next? I immediately reinvested every penny into my business, buying exercise equipment, dumbbells, kettlebells, exercise balls, mats, etc. Up to that point, I had trained the few people who had walked into my bootcamp, just using body weight exercises.

As the saying goes, "If you're going to fail, do so fast and cheap."

And I'll be honest. At that point, my self-esteem was at an all-time low. I seriously believed, when I opened the first location of my gym in September 2010, I'd be closed by Christmas.

It was only after the success of several subsequent LivingSocial deals (and Groupon, who eventually accepted me) that my self-belief and confidence grew. In just a matter of two-

and-a-half years, I was training classes of over eighty-plus people by myself.

Little ol' insecure Johnny, after placing his gym less than a mile from both Gold's Gym and Planet Fitness, had somehow created a "Mega Bootcamp." The reason I'm telling you this story is for two very important lessons I want you to implement into your life's journey.

Lesson 1: The first lesson is the importance of forward movement and being resourceful.

To reiterate what I mentioned previously, all human beings are more driven by pain than we are by pleasure. Which means, if taking action is scarier than remaining where you are, we shouldn't be surprised if nothing ever changes.

Things changed for me when my fear of remaining the old version of me became scarier than moving forward into the uncertain future.

Take this, for example: I'd been attempting to quit my habit of cracking my knuckles for years. Every year, I'd put the task of quitting on my yearly goal list. And every year, I'd fail.

I was literally driving home from church one Sunday morning when I received a brilliant idea. So, before I had a chance to overthink it, I flipped on a Facebook Live video and began to broadcast. This is how it went.

> *"Friends, what's up? Johnny here, and I need your help! I've been wanting to stop cracking my knuckles for years. And this week is when it's going to happen. For the first five people who comment below this video, I am giving you my word that I will pay you $500 each if I don't stop cracking my knuckles by the end of the day on Wednesday.*
>
> *How will you know if I'm being honest? You won't. This is my word. And I am promising you an update first thing on Thursday what my outcome is."*

Sure as shit, I had so many people comment and cheer me on. So many people said this was a brilliant idea to gain leverage for breaking a bad habit. And what happened? I completed my goal of stopping that bad habit prior to Wednesday night.

Why? Because the idea of losing $2,500 became way more painful than the pain of knuckle-cracking withdrawal.

So, this is why you've got to stack the deck in your favor. And you do that by making remaining where you currently are more painful than moving forward.

Most people won't go on a diet, change their spending habits, or go to marriage counseling until they have a major health scare, run out of money, or have a spouse threaten to leave. This is absolutely why—as has become a recurring theme—the enemy of greatness in men is the temptation to settle for "good enough."

If you feel as though you don't have what it takes to make change last or if you've taken action in the past but come up short, then I challenge you to become more resourceful. This is precisely why I used Facebook (which is a free resource) to connect with people I didn't know and to hold me accountable to quitting a bad habit.

Lesson 2: The second lesson is that guidance and accountability create leverage worth its price in gold.

For instance, there was a weekend early in my gym ownership days when I was majorly stressed. I had hit a threshold where I knew I was going to have more clients on Monday morning's class than I had equipment for.

My belief was that every client had to all do the same exercise at the same time. I was nearly ready to go drop several thousand more dollars on workout equipment.

I'm grateful that the thought came to me to ask my business coach, Steve, if he had any advice. I'll tell you what, hiring him was the best decision I could have made at the time. Because he instructed me in the simple art of people movement, by implementing a special kind of format that incorporated the use of multiple exercise stations.

Overnight, my classes went from overwhelming and disorganized to a beautifully orchestrated dance of masses of clientele, all of whom all knew where they were going, and when and what they needed to do.

I learned that weekend, when it comes to sticking points in life, the solution can often be gained either by time or money. You can waste time by learning painful lessons by going through them personally, or...

You can spend money to hire someone who can teach you solutions in a matter of minutes that may otherwise take you months or *years* of struggle to learn firsthand.

You can always make more money. However, you cannot buy more time. This is precisely why I'll always find resourceful ways of coming up with money to pay for amazing coaching.

One pitfall to be aware of is this: your ego may justify that it's important for you to accomplish something all on your own, without asking for support or guidance. Unfortunately, that's a recipe for wasted time and a wasted life.

You heard it here first.

CHAPTER 9

The Calling

"One can have no smaller or greater mastery than mastery of oneself."

—Leonardo da Vinci

The 3 Kingdoms of Mastery

HAVE YOU EVER experienced a day where everything was perfect from start to finish?

I remember experiencing this once when I was in college, during a summer break. A friend and I had driven to the home of his parents who lived on this pristine and beautiful lake, in order to spend the day water skiing and tubing.

There were patches of fog that morning that hovered atop the surface of the water as we fired up the engine to his parents' boat. The first several runs were epic. The water was smooth as glass, and as I carved the wake board and slalom ski back and forth from side to side, I knew it was going to be a good day.

By the end, it was beyond good. We skied, BBQed, laid out in the sun, talked, laughed, and went tubing.

I reflected back on the day in that last golden hour, before the sun dipped below the horizon. I still absolutely love that time of day, when the color of the sun becomes a honeyed hue, and the intensity of sunlight isn't strong enough to hurt my slightly burned skin.

There I sat at the end of the dock, dipping my feet in the water with three of my best friends, quietly basking in the sun, and the thought popped into my mind, *Does life get any better than this?*

In some ways, life doesn't get much easier than when you're twenty-one and can do whatever you want, while not having any of the pressures of a proper adult's life (like a mortgage, bills, having to work a fulltime adult job, etc.).

I enjoy thinking back on many similar moments, because I want to experience the feeling I had at the end of that day more often. My aim is to feel that sense of accomplishment, that I've truly lived my best life, as often as I can. Now, just to be clear, it's a lot easier to "live your best life" when you're on vacation, so I'm in pursuit of that feeling during a typical work day.

I want to look back at my life and be able to say I played full-out, that I gave it hell, and I was proud of how I played this game of life. Leaving it all on the field.

There has to be a standard of excellence in everything we do in our lives, as men.

This is what the concept of *Becoming Kings* is all about.

You have the power to change the trajectory of how men have been showing up in past generations. You and I, we have the opportunity and the responsibility to accept what has worked and to change what needs improvement.

There's so much that is amazing about being a man. And yet, there have been plenty of men who—out of their wounds and pain—have given the rest of us a bad name.

So, the question is, how exactly do you want to show up as a man? How do you want to be remembered? To conquer and reign over your own life instead of being at its mercy, you've got to define what it means for you to become a King.

The journey of Becoming Kings begins with reigning over the following 3 Kingdoms of your life:

THE 3 KINGDOMS OF MASTERY

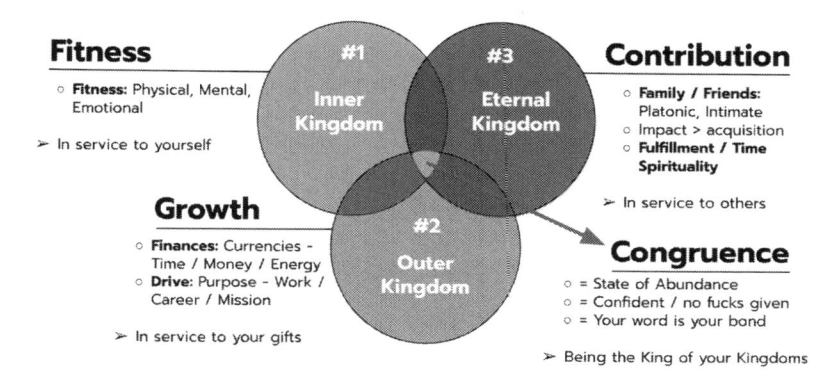

Fitness
- Fitness: Physical, Mental, Emotional
- ➤ In service to yourself

Growth
- Finances: Currencies - Time / Money / Energy
- Drive: Purpose - Work / Career / Mission
- ➤ In service to your gifts

Contribution
- Family / Friends: Platonic, Intimate
- Impact > acquisition
- Fulfillment / Time Spirituality
- ➤ In service to others

Congruence
- = State of Abundance
- = Confident / no fucks given
- = Your word is your bond
- ➤ Being the King of your Kingdoms

#1 Inner Kingdom
#2 Outer Kingdom
#3 Eternal Kingdom

The first of the three Kingdoms you must conquer is your **Inner Kingdom**. It's arguably the most important of all the Kingdoms, since you cannot support others if you are not healthy in mind, body, and emotions.

The second is your **Outer Kingdom,** which is all about the magnification of your gifts. This area of life is all about what you are committed to building in your life. By utilizing your divine gifts, the sky's the limit for how much good you can do in the world.

The third is your **Eternal Kingdom.** This is where you take all the wisdom and humility you've garnered from a lifetime of success and learning, and you pay it forward to your lover, your family, friends, community, and to the world.

In the middle of these 3 Kingdoms—where you see them overlapping—is where congruence is found.

When you have abundance in all three Kingdoms, that's where a King can be found.

I am reminded of a story I'll not soon forget. Shortly before my mom passed away, I was sitting at the end of her bed after swinging by to see her after work. My sister and my father were there beside her, also.

We had been having a good conversation, although it was clear my mom was in tremendous pain. I sat there, rubbing her feet, which isn't something I would have normally done. And yet, seeing her in so much pain and feeling powerless to change anything, it was the least I could do to comfort her.

I sat there for an hour, attempting to make light conversation between her coughing fits, when she'd throw up, gasping for air and struggling to regain her breath. My sister and I did everything we could to comfort her.

That's when the anger within reached an all-time high.

My dad was also sitting next to my mom, head down, on his phone. And all I can remember that particular day was the rage I felt. The interesting thing is, though, underneath all of that rage was the sadness and grief I had been suppressing.

In my podcast interview with the always-insightful coach and author, Christine Hassler, she explained, "I believe a lot of men think that emotions, that kind of release and tears, are less manly. When nothing could be further from the truth.

"That's why it is so, so important for men to feel safe to express not only their rage but their tears. If we're making generalizations, the flip of that is women can be more comfortable with tears and need to get to their rage.

"Usually, for men, getting to their rage is easier and the grief is harder, and it's the flip for women. Again, massive generalization, but it's what I have seen after sixteen years of doing this. And for men, often it is the anger that unlocks the grief, and for women it's the grief that unlocks the anger."

I couldn't agree with her more. What I didn't know at the time (and would learn years later) was there was a *much* bigger elephant in the room that day, one I was unaware of. As I sat there, doing what I could to comfort my mom, I was also keenly aware that my father sat next to her, messing around on his phone. The mistake I made that day was to assign a negative meaning to my father's behavior.

What could have served me was to ask, "What else could this mean?"

At the time, the meaning I assigned to my father's actions was that he couldn't care less for me, for my siblings, or for my mom. And yet, that couldn't have been further from the truth. He now tells me, in that moment, he felt so powerless, just as I had, and he was doing all he could to distract himself and keep from falling apart emotionally.

I now have the perspective to see that my father did the best he could with the tools he had at the time. However, in the moment, by my mother's bedside, a lifetime of bitterness, anger, and resentment that had accumulated toward him was beginning to boil over.

Those several years after my mom passed away became a long grieving process of letting go of how I *"thought"* my life should have been versus accepting it as how it was. I had to let die the belief my life "should" have been any different than the way it was, and only after a lot of radical honesty did my life dramatically change.

I finally saw it wasn't only my mother who had been starved of the love she ultimately needed. So did my father.

For all that my parents didn't get from each other emotionally, they poured it into other pursuits. For my mom, it was her five kids. For my father, it was his business and providing for his family financially. They avoided talking about the elephant in the room within their relationship, and they over-compensated, with my mom becoming a "momaholic" and my dad, a "workaholic."

What they lacked in romantic love, they made up for by settling for the breadcrumbs of connecting over a mutual love of us children, travel and food, which, in turn, led to their unhealthy lifestyle. My mom was roughly seventy pounds overweight, and, at the time of her passing, my dad was overweight by 120 pounds.

Why I bring up this story is because it illustrates a great example of how intertwined all three Kingdoms are in our lives.

If you do not create a strong foundation by achieving mastery over the first of the three kingdoms, you will never be able to fully experience life—no matter how much money, success, and amazing relationships you have.

You cannot reign over all three kingdoms until you systematically create abundance within you, by becoming mentally, emotionally, and physically fit. The limitations you accept as to what you can achieve with your physical, mental, and emotional health will be the bottleneck to your experience of abundance in all other facets of life.

CHAPTER 10

Your Inner Kingdom

"Champions aren't made in the gyms. Champions are made from something they have deep inside them—a desire, a dream, a vision."

—Muhammad Ali

IN MY TEN-PLUS years of coaching all across the world, it's been interesting to see the patterns that hold people back from achieving their goals. More times than not, the reason people struggle with achieving what they want is because they don't feel worthy of it.

Their identity or idea of themselves holds them hostage from the limitless possibilities of what they could become.

Your results in life are a direct reflection of your standards, and your standards are a direct reflection of your self-worth. To achieve fulfillment in life, you must achieve emotional and mental abundance.

The next logical question is, "How does one improve his self-worth and self-esteem?"

Let's think about this logically.

There have, no doubt, been many things in your life you weren't good at, initially, yet now you take them completely for granted, as skills. How did you accomplish those things?

Truth be told, proficiency in anything comes as the result of practice. Over and over and over again, you practiced riding your bike or tying your shoe or learning to speak clearly and accurately. The only challenge is you've forgotten this was the path to confidence.

When you were a little guy, you didn't second-guess yourself as to whether walking, talking, running, riding a bike, or tying your shoes was something you wanted to pursue. You inherently knew it was part of being independent. So, even though it was hard as hell and you failed over and over again, you didn't give up.

Over time, eventually you got better. To the point where what were once dreams are now realities you again take for granted.

But that is the formula for building confidence and self-esteem. To build esteem for yourself, you must do the things you know you must, even if they're hard. And chances are they will be very hard and you will want to quit.

My longtime friend and now mentor, Lewis Howes, explained his strategy on an episode of my podcast, about how he went about increasing his skills and confidence.

He said, "If you want a strategy to increase skills and confidence, something I did from an early age was I would create a list of my top fears of the year. Early on, it was speaking in public, because I was always intimidated in school, speaking aloud. I was scared to dance in public and salsa dance. I was scared to learn an instrument. And I just said, okay, whatever my biggest fears are, I'm going to set out and do them this year.

"So, one year I did toastmasters, where I went to public speaking class every week for a year, and I was horrible and embarrassed and the worst person there, until I wasn't. Until I practiced so much, I became better. Same thing with salsa dancing. I was terrified of being in the middle of a dance floor when I didn't understand the music or the dance. But doing it every single day for three and a half months and obsessing over it, I finally overcame the fear. And then I became pretty good! And then it was fun!

"So, this thing that used to cause me fear is now fun! Because it took so many hours of practice to overcome the fear, I'm no longer afraid anymore. When you're afraid of something, it's not fun. But when you conquer the fear through your actual actions and the work and time it took you to do it, you feel proud of yourself, and that pride turns into fulfillment.

"It became fun to speak in public as opposed to fearful and terrifying. It became fun to go salsa dancing as opposed to being embarrassing when every girl would reject me.

"So, whatever your fear is, go in on the fear until it disappears, and that will now become a skill you can use forever. Yes, double down on your strengths *and* do the thing that causes you fear until it no longer cripples you. It's no longer a kryptonite when someone comes to you and asks, 'Okay, Lewis, can you speak aloud in front for this presentation?'

"When you do this, you become recession-proof, bulletproof, and your confidence increases massively! Compare that to if you go all in on what you're already good at, your confidence increases only a little bit. Because you're already really good at it. You can only get a little further on it every day or month. But when you see a jump in something that you're horrible at, to, 'man, I'm actually not that horrible at this anymore,' your confidence increases ten times, a hundred times, on that *and* everything else in your life.

"So, whatever it is, I would say write a list of your biggest fears and start tackling them one at a time."

It's inevitable: as we grow older, and basic things become second nature, we come to believe that most things—even new things—shouldn't be hard. Or that we should be proficient at something prior to attempting it, otherwise it's not worth the risk. And yet, that thought process is faulty.

The first step in creating life abundance and fulfillment is getting clear on what it is you want to achieve. I'll dive into this deeper later in the book. However, fundamentally, it's impossible to make progress until you know where you're headed.

If you haven't picked up on it yet, a big part of becoming the King of your life is *intentionality*.

If you aren't intentional and you allow yourself to drift through life day by day, who knows where you'll end up? Chances are good you'll awaken some day in the middle of the ocean, after spending a lifetime adrift. And you'll wonder, "How did I let myself get here?"

One of the purposes of this book is to support you, so you can avoid that ever happening to you.

Creating abundance means you make decisions that are in alignment with who you are committed to being and what you want to create in the future. You do not make decisions that are out of alignment with your goals or incongruent with this way of being a King.

Here's a little piece of advice, especially if you've found yourself as a recovering "nice guy," "yes man," or "people pleaser":

Countless individuals I've worked with over the years have felt, in order to take time for themselves—whether it be to work out, to meditate, to create time for whatever it is *they* need to feel emotionally fulfilled—they're required to be selfish.

This mindset can be especially pervasive if you have other people in your life. A spouse, kids, family, demanding work—

whatever the outside priority is, it's understandable one could feel selfish or scared to take time just for themselves.

I want you to think about the word "selfish" in a different context. When someone is perceived as being "selfish," it's typically because they're seen to be hoarding something for themselves, instead of offering it to others.

The word "selfish" is just a fancy cover-up for someone who is feeling extremely fearful and worried they're going to lose something. So, their reaction is to hold on to whatever they can get their hands on.

Rather than be scared of being deemed selfish, you've got to be willing to flip the script on what you're *really* scared of.

Instead of being fearful of missing out on time with your family because you prioritize forty-five minutes for working out, become more scared of losing your health and having a subpar quality of life, because you didn't take care of yourself.

Instead of worrying you'll be judged by others, if you leave work an hour before they do, hold steadfast and confident that the hour you gain by going to the gym or heading home at a decent hour to see your spouse and kids is time you'll never be able to buy back.

In many ways, we as men can easily slip into a rut of complacency and mediocrity, the older we get. There's a common belief out there that, as you age, there's less motivation to take care of yourself, your relationships, etc. Because we ask ourselves, "What's the point? I'm no longer in my prime. I'm over the hill."

It's a lot like the analogy of the frog that sits in water as it slowly heats, and who doesn't feel the effects of the increase in temperature until it's too late and it has boiled to death. We're the same way. Over time, the slow dimming of healthy habits can have a massive negative ripple effect across your entire life.

This is precisely why building a strong foundation of your Inner Kingdom is so vitally important.

To illustrate what happens when a man doesn't take his physical, mental, and emotional health seriously, let's look closer at the impacts of bad habits in this hypothetical scenario of a made-up character we'll call "Larry."

Ever since Larry was young, he used to spend quality time with his mom, baking amazing food for their family. Muffins, cookies, cakes, you name it—they baked it.

Now, as an adult, Larry spends a lot of time watching the Food Channel and making amazing food. He does this because it reminds him of the time he spent with his mother. Whenever his wife and family all get together for the holidays or special occasions, his siblings put in their special baking requests.

Just like when he was little, after he bakes, once it comes hot out of the oven, he ends up sampling a little more than his fair share of the finished product.

Over the years, Larry notices how his slow and steady weight gain has been catching up to him. More times than not, he wakes up groggy and feeling like he's been hit by a bus. Throughout his day, he uses caffeine and sugary food to give him quick hits of energy. However, they don't last long.

His crankiness and sleep deprivation start to take their toll on both his relationships with coworkers as well as his performance at work. Every afternoon, he struggles to keep his eyes open. More than once, when walking by, his boss has awoken him, because Larry has nodded off at his desk. All of these little slippages of performance have warranted several conversations with his boss about how he needs to step up his game and productivity.

When he gets home, Larry's wife is excited to see him and asks how his day was. While yawning, he has a really difficult time remembering what he even accomplished that day while at work, so their conversation is short-lived. Knowing he's struggling, he grabs from the cookie jar a few cookies he baked earlier this past weekend and sits down in front of the TV to numb out for a little.

On multiple occasions, Larry's wife has asked him to go for a walk around the neighborhood like they used to. However, his overall lack of energy makes it a lot more difficult to get motivated. She begins to wonder where the man she married has disappeared to. Because he seems less interested in doing things with her like they used to, she seeks out other friends and activities to fill her time.

Larry begins to feel like he's living out real-life scenes from the movie *Groundhog Day*, where Bill Murray wakes up each morning to live the same day over and over again. Larry gets so bored with his life he loathes the idea of going to bed, only to wake up and live the same day on repeat. So, he stays up late, eating more crap food, before eventually falling asleep on the couch in front of the TV.

The more he eats, the less energy he has, and the less motivation he feels. More and more often, his growing anger boils over. He finds himself snapping about the littlest of things, criticizing his wife, kids, family members, and co-workers.

Within this continued downward spiral, the number on the scale continues to grow. And with his weight gain, Larry feels less confident, attractive, and romantic. With fewer meaningful conversations, compliments, and physical intimacy with his wife, she emotionally withdraws and pours her energy into her job and the kids.

Although he knows she's extremely lonely, he is, too. And at this point, they're both doing the best they can just to keep their heads above water, while avoiding blowing up into stress-related bickering. Feeling emotionally starved, Larry's wife finds herself liking the subtle flirtatious advances made by one of her co-workers.

Seeing the writing on the wall, she requests they go to marriage counseling. He dismisses it by minimizing her feelings and rationalizing that marriage counseling is only for couples who can't figure out their own problems. Instead, Larry believes a lot of their marital problems are his wife's fault.

Rather than looking within and doing the necessary work to clean up his own mess, Larry avoids taking responsibility for his own bad habits. He's not aware of the ripple effect of the small, shitty choices he made over time that gained momentum, rolling into a huge snowball of blame and fault-finding...

Although this is a hypothetical scenario, you know as well as I do how many millions of men are living this life. As subtly as life can take a downward turn due to the accumulation of small bad choices, the same is true for making small incremental improvements that result in positive changes in your life. With enough time and consistency, making small changes will have a profoundly positive impact upon your Kingdoms.

This is not brain surgery. Often, success principles are not new ideas to us. They become clichés because the things that brought men into greatness hundreds and thousands of years ago are no different than they are now.

Each and every man who has ever left a positive and enriching legacy has done so by—first and foremost—taking responsibility for who they are, how they behave, and what they accomplish in life.

This is the fundamental principle of building the foundation of your Inner Kingdom on solid ground. By leapfrogging over the difficult work of integrating self-love within your Inner Kingdom, everything you create will be built upon an unstable foundation.

This is precisely why you must face your demons. And this is done daily, on a moment-to-moment basis. You are no help to anyone if you don't first take care of yourself.

Which brings me to an important point: I cannot stress enough how important it is that you have an evening and morning ritual. By finishing the day strong, you're able to start the next day strong.

So many "successful people" talk about how important and necessary their morning ritual is. However, if you do not create consistency at night, then chances are great you'll be way too exhausted to get up early in the morning.

When you're too exhausted in the morning, you hit the snooze one too many times. Then, the rest of the day often feels like you're just battling to catch back up to where the rest of the world is. It can feel like a self-imposed one-hour penalty to the daily race, where everyone else is already ahead of you. And truthfully, it's the worst fucking feeling.

The alternative is like a gift to yourself. So, this is how I recommend you approach your evening so you can get high-quality sleep and, thus, be on your game first thing in the morning.

CHAPTER 11

Evening & Morning Routines for Men

"Be boring and orderly in your life, so that you may be violent and original in your work."

—Gustave Flaubert

Creating a Fulfilling Evening Routine

THERE ARE LOTS of simple-to-use, free apps available. I recommend you download one to your phone, to keep track of your healthy habits each and every day.

My recommendation is, if you have never implemented an evening routine, you ease your way into it, rather than bite off more than you can chew. I'm a big believer that when it comes to rituals, more is less. A very common pattern in people is to allow the thought of positive change to excite us. That can lead, unfortunately, to our transitioning into a new habit too quickly, which can overwhelm us as we attempt to do too much too fast.

Speaking from experience, starting off with executing on an evening or morning routine that is no longer than fifteen minutes is perfect. Otherwise, it's easy to fall victim to feeling overwhelmed.

If it's longer than fifteen minutes, I often feel it's too much time, and I'll put it off until later that day or the next. So, take it from me, and heed this piece of advice...

When it comes to habit creation, consistency is way more important than quantity.

Most everyone has some sort of basic evening ritual, such as brushing their teeth, washing their face, etc. And that's a solid start. One thing that makes a huge difference for me is I set a bedtime and try to hit it consistently. Personally, I like to aim to be in bed by 9 p.m., so I can read for at least ten minutes. This also means that waking up at 5-6 a.m. is also reasonable.

If I go to bed after 10 p.m., chances of me needing to sleep until 6 or 7 a.m. become more likely.

For my evening ritual, I like to have three to five things on my list. And it looks like this:

1. Be getting ready for bed by 9 p.m. at the latest.
2. No streaming of anything video related for at least an hour prior to bed.
3. Define tomorrow's top-three things that must be done, and schedule them into my calendar.
4. Ten minutes of reading.
5. Three gratitudes from the day, before falling asleep

Of course, my normal hygiene ritual is in there, too. However, I don't count it against my fifteen minutes, because it's a given. And I never need prompting to remember to brush my teeth.

What are those things that may not be healthy habits, ones you might want to break? For me, if I start watching Netflix, then I could ultimately watch hours of it and not turn it off until midnight or 1 a.m. When this happens, it's not healthy at all.

That's why one of my evening rituals is to ensure I'm not watching any Netflix or streaming video for the hour prior to going to sleep. I have gone so far as to delete the apps off my phone and other devices during the week, in order to create resistance to just turning on a show while brushing my teeth.

Studies have shown how much improved rest you receive, when your brain isn't stimulated by a digital device prior to sleeping.

So, I want you to take a moment and write out a rough draft of your evening routine. Don't fall into the trap of thinking your evening routine needs to be perfect, because, honestly, I'm constantly tweaking mine.

What's most important is:

* You go to bed at a consistent time, and
* You know before going to bed what you need to accomplish tomorrow.

When I was working in corporate America, I'd have my top-three things to do tomorrow figured out even earlier, usually prior to my leaving work for the day. The key to having your day dialed in and being productive is ensuring you get quality sleep.

For instance, I found online—which *must* mean that it's all 100% true (insert sarcasm here)—this short list of problems associated with a lack of sleep:

- 23.3% of adults report poorer concentration
- 18.2% of adults report forgetfulness
- 13.3% of adults report neglecting hobbies
- 11.3% of adults report difficulty driving
- 10.5% of adults report neglecting financial affairs
- 8.6% of adults report work interference

Compare those figures to what the National Sleep Foundation identified in adults who get an average of seven to nine hours of sleep:

- Recharges the brain
- Consolidates learning
- Releases important hormones
- Repairs your cells

Logically, if you're not getting ample quality sleep, so your body is able to replenish itself, how long can you go until every performance-based activity in your life is deeply impacted?

This is why I am a huge stickler about sleep. I have blackout shades in my bedroom, an amazingly comfortable mattress, and I always ensure it's cold enough. I cannot sleep well when my bedroom is too hot.

Another thing that makes a massive difference is the placement of my phone at night. If I keep it next to my bed, I'm 100% more likely to use it from my bed. Not to mention, I'm 100% more likely also to snooze the alarm, rather than immediately get up in the morning.

One of my simple life hacks, something I highly recommend, is to keep your phone somewhere else other than beside you. This way, when the alarm goes off, you have to get up and out of bed to shut it off. Just that amount of effort is often enough to free you from snoozing your morning away.

Now that the evening routine is squared away, let's move on to...

Creating a Powerful Morning Routine

Once I'm up and out of bed, I immediately get into my morning ritual. A big focus we should all have is to feel like we're immediately succeeding. I recommend you plan things on your morning-ritual checklist that are easily completed and make you feel accomplished.

For instance, the first thing I always do is use the bathroom. So? That's one of the first few items on my list. And why not? Once I get into it, the momentum builds, and item after item is checked off. Using the bathroom is a trigger for me to begin checking things off my list. Here's what my morning ritual looks like:

- Get up. No snooze. (If I do this, it's already a great day!)
- No social media for the first hour of being awake
- Use the bathroom
- Put on my Apple watch
- Brush teeth
- 16 ounces of alkaline water
- 30 push-ups
- 50 sit-ups
- Make the bed
- Meditation

Even if that's all I do, for me, that's a great start to get my body awake and ready to take on the day. If you're just beginning, I wouldn't start with much more than that. Why? Because—again—I believe momentum is everything. So, get yourself into a routine, and bang it out for at least twenty-one days. Once you feel like you've really dialed in what works for you, then you can build upon it.

I have set up my house with the bare essentials, so I can accomplish my first tasks before leaving my room. Once I go downstairs to the kitchen, I have another set of rituals I like to accomplish. These involve more push-ups, sit-ups, jumping on my mini-trampoline, watching something motivational on YouTube, doing visualization, praying, affirmations, etc.

If this is helpful, I recommend you take a moment and either:

* Create your first morning ritual, or
* If you already have one, ask yourself how you can dial it in even further. What's working for you, and what isn't?

This isn't just a question to ask yourself as it relates to your morning and evening rituals. It applies to all areas of your life. How are your nutrition and supplementation, your workouts, your happiness, and your stress levels? Does your body feel good? Or does it feel tight and old?

As I've said before, and you'll hear me say it again, how you do anything is how you do everything. Wherever your mental state is, on a regular basis, your physical health will mirror it.

You *must* become the King of your Inner Kingdom first and foremost, because self-discipline begins with the mastery of your thoughts. If you don't control what you think, you can't control what you do.

It's not only what you do but how people experience you that will be the legacy you leave. Side note: this is just the tip of the iceberg to what I would recommend as it relates to evening and morning rituals. If you need more in-depth support, go to my website, JohnnyKing.com, and check out my programs. I've got inexpensive and highly effective solutions to help you time manage and win the day.

Once you have dominion over your Inner Kingdom, over your physical, mental, and emotional health, you will find you have a huge increase in space and bandwidth to focus on your Outer Kingdom.

CHAPTER 12

Your Outer Kingdom

"If you want to find your purpose in life, find your wound."
—Rick Warren

YOUR OUTER KINGDOM consists of what your life's purpose is.

Over the past decade of coaching, when talking with men and women, I can determine a lot about how much their work means to them by what type of language they use to describe it. For instance, do they talk about their job, a career, or a mission they're committed to?

The words you use to describe your work say a lot about the intention, purpose, and heart behind it—or the lack thereof.

Years ago, I was a part of Tony Robbins's Platinum Partnership, where I was assigned a high-end coach, Dr. Keith Waggoner, for the year. He is a Godly man, and one I highly respect. During one of our weekly coaching calls, he asked me, "Have you ever seen the movie, *The Passion of the Christ?*"

I had seen it when it first came out. However, I didn't remember much of it other than the brutal depiction of Christ's crucifixion.

He went on to explain that, nowadays, people most often inaccurately define the word "passion" as something they are excited about.

I, too, had gotten accustomed to asking about men's passions for what they do. Did they have a level of excitement and commitment to their work, to their relationship with their spouse, etc.?

However, Coach Keith said something that day that resonated deeply. He went on to tell me...,

"Johnny, *The Passion of the Christ* is a movie all about Jesus's willingness to suffer and die for what he believed in. It doesn't matter whether you're religious or not. The point is it was Jesus's 'passion' that allowed him to sacrifice his own wellbeing for the greater good. When people find their 'passion,' it is often characterized by a willingness to sacrifice— their time, their comfort, their money, their comfortable life— for something that has greater impact."

This made a ton of sense. When you really think about it, people who are passionate about something are often willing to sacrifice their time, blood, sweat, and tears toward their endeavor.

This is exactly what the Outer Kingdom is about. It's about defining your drive in life and what you're passionately contributing and growing toward.

Where I got this all wrong is, for much of my life (until I was roughly thirty years old), I had made women out to be the prize I was willing to sacrifice for. All through high school, college and my twenties, I was willing to sacrifice my happiness for the significance I received by being whatever they wanted me to be.

I mean, it makes sense. I was raised primarily by women, so their validation was where I found my sense of identity. To make my mom, my teachers, and my girlfriend happy made me feel like I had value. However, the older I got, the wiser I became to the fact that it was neither within my power, nor my responsibility to "make a woman happy."

This is precisely why you, first and foremost, must establish your Inner Kingdom—so no matter how many curveballs life throws your way, you cannot be shaken.

Understanding what makes you happy, fulfilled, and passionate is what leads to being unshakable.

Over the years, as I've become more and more clear about my life's purpose, the validation I once sought from the opposite sex has dissipated. I've become more focused on impact instead of affirmation. I say this because the way I now show up in intimate relationships is drastically different than how I did years ago.

For instance, have you ever been in a relationship with someone who was extremely needy? Like their happiness depended upon you giving them your attention, validation, and flattery? It's exhausting, is it not? Well, I've been on both sides of the equation, being needed and being needy.

There's a position being taken by many these days that is extremely pervasive and destructive. With it, people like to say, "Oh, I don't *need* a woman," or "I don't *need* a man. I'm complete just as I am." However, it's my opinion that there is nothing wrong with needing another person. To share life together. To magnify all there is to experience in this one precious life.

The difference between neediness and needing someone is, for the needy, their insecurity drives their behavior. They struggle to acknowledge their own self-worth because they're too distracted by the thoughts, feelings, and opinions others have of them.

Those who need another human being know they are on a journey, a life trajectory that is enhanced by, but not dependent upon, the validation of another or others.

For me, it has taken the better part of forty years to reach the point where I only have so many fucks to give about what others think of me. I'm very focused on building my Outer Kingdom in a way I believe it should be built.

When we circle back around to the *Science of Achievement* and the *Art of Fulfillment*, the question you must ask yourself is: "If I could create my ideal lifestyle, what would it *really* look like?"

Because there are specific currencies you get to invest in that allow you to zero in on what your ideal lifestyle looks like. These currencies are like levers you can push and pull to get different outcomes.

Typically, when anyone mentions the term "currency," our first thought goes to...

Money

The vast majority of the working class trades their time, working a job or providing a service. That service is rewarded with money, which they use to buy goods—food, utilities, shelter, clothing, transportation, etc.

The challenge is they're making a trade. They're trading time for money. Which brings us to the second currency, which is...

Time

Make no mistake: time is the far more valuable of the two. It's the one thing you can never buy more of, no matter how wealthy you are.

And what *is* time really? Have you ever thought about it?

What I've learned is that time is affixed to emotion. For instance, when you're sitting in a dentist's chair, does time fly by or does it drag? When you're late and stuck in traffic on your way to the airport, so you can get out of town with your significant other for the weekend, each five-minute increment can seem like an hour. So, when you're not enjoying yourself, time moves like molasses.

Compare that to when you're having a blast, in an amazing conversation, hanging out with friends, or on an incredible date. Time flies.

So, when you're experiencing positive emotions, time flies. And when you're experiencing painful emotions, time passes extremely slowly.

The third and final currency you must learn to work for your advantage is...

Energy

And if you don't take care of yourself physically, what happens? Horrible eating habits lead to weight gain. When you are overweight and increasing the burden on your system, it takes more horsepower and, thus, more fuel to achieve the same result.

So, it's a downward spiral, if you don't have your nutrition and exercise routines dialed in. The further your unhealthy physical habits spiral, the lower your energy levels dip.

Imagine someone like Larry, from earlier. Someone who is overweight and unhealthy. Do they get home ready, excited, and full of energy from the work they've done during the day? Or is it the opposite?

Countless men get home each day physically and emotionally drained, angry, and depressed. Do you think they have any excitement or passion to inject into their interactions with loved ones?

Of course not. They're emotionally flatlined. And guess who bears the brunt of that emptiness besides them? Their spouse, their kids, and their loved ones.

Which brings us to the third and final Kingdom...

CHAPTER 13

Your Eternal Kingdom

"I want us all to fulfill our greatest potential. To find our calling, and summon the courage to live it."

—Oprah Winfrey

WHENEVER SOMETHING incredible happens in your life—whether it's a promotion, you receive an award, you win tickets to a concert—whatever the case...what's the first thing you do, when something great happens to you?

Chances are you immediately pick up the phone and call someone you love to share the news with them!

Why is this? It's because our lives are magnified through the sharing of it with other people we love.

During the COVID pandemic, it was eerie to watch sporting events on the TV when there weren't any fans. And it was even weirder when they attempt to put in fake images or sounds of fans.

So, just imagine you are the only person in the stands of an MMA fight, at a concert of your favorite band, or in Times Square celebrating the ball dropping on New Year's Eve. Point being, it can be extremely lonely to experience life by yourself.

All of the aforementioned events are magnified when sharing them with a massive crowd of passionate and excited fans. This is precisely why being in proximity to others is so important to our lives.

For many men and women, even though they would absolutely love to spend more time at home with their significant other and kids, the pressure to provide becomes more valuable. Countless individuals feel increasing guilt as their young children grow without much presence of their parent or parents, who are busy working to support the family.

I remember feeling this way, too, when I was younger. The more I worked, the more money I made—all of which magnified the feelings of significance and pride about the lifestyle I had created. The more money I made, the nicer the cars, the nicer the homes, and so on.

The more I worked, the more recognition I got at work, the more people respected me, and the more important I felt. It was like a drug. And yet the lack of time I spent at home meant my relationship suffered. I was making a choice to trade one for the other.

As these three Kingdoms continue to build upon one another, you will find they all share a symbiotic relationship. Like a three-legged stool, without all three Kingdoms working together, the other two will certainly fall.

This is why the third and final Kingdom is so important.

The Eternal Kingdom is where all the juice in life is. It rests on the shoulders of the Inner and Outer Kingdoms. Like the foundation of a skyscraper, without the physical, emotional, and mental strength, you will never have the longevity to pour yourself fully into your life's purpose and the relationships that matter most.

Without the sense of confidence and humility that comes from being a man who knows his purpose, chances will increase that you will ultimately find yourself "lost," "stuck," and "lonely" in life without it.

By having the combination of a strong physical body, along with the mental fortitude that comes from being a man on purpose, you'll have the ability to contribute and be present to the relationships that matter most.

It's our relationships, both platonic and intimate, that determine the quality of our lives. There's no sum of money or a number on the scale that can replace the joy that comes from cultivating amazing relationships with those in your circle.

Another way to think about the three Kingdoms is as concentric circles.

When you throw a stone into a pond, the water ripples out in concentric circles. The innermost circle is the Inner Kingdom, where the focus is when you're in service to yourself. The next circle is that of your Outer Kingdom, where the focus is when you're in service of sharing your gifts with the world. And the outermost circle is that of your Eternal Kingdom, where the focus is when you're in service to others.

Previously, I mentioned the concept of the *Science of Achievement* and the *Art of Fulfillment*. It's very easy for a man to focus all his efforts into the Outer Kingdom, where he can fulfill his need for significance.

The issue countless men run into is their desire to make money or build a business puts them at risk of losing either or both their physical health and the health of their relationship(s).

This is the result of being a one-dimensional man. Being one-dimensional is only focusing on reigning over one of the three Kingdoms, while the health of the other two Kingdoms starves.

Only by being a three-dimensional man can you find the sweet spot, where all three Kingdoms overlap and congruence is experienced.

In your pursuit of Becoming a King and experiencing all the abundance life has to offer, congruence is a prerequisite. Congruence is the balance between the confidence of knowing who you are and the humility of no longer needing to prove yourself to anyone. It's a place where you know your opinions about things, yet you're still open to hearing what other people think.

Alison Armstrong is the author of international bestsellers, *Keys to the Kingdom* and *In Sync With the Opposite Sex* (as well as the creator of UnderstandingMen.com). During our interview on my podcast, she said:

"In summary, congruence is when your word aligns with your actions. If you say you will do something, you do it. Your word is your bond."

Fulfillment comes from a life of constant growth, contribution, and a commitment to serving others more today than you did yesterday.

Without having dialed in your fitness, your finances, your purpose in life, your relationships with your family, friends, and your faith, fulfillment of living abundantly will be difficult to achieve.

For me, my spiritual journey has not been one without its ups and downs. I'm not about to tell you what you should or shouldn't believe. However, I am confident my accomplishments would not have been possible without a belief in a higher creator, what I refer to as God.

If you don't believe in God or a higher Creator, you are 100% entitled to your beliefs. What I have found difficult, personally, is to see how perfect everything fits together in nature and not believe there is a higher creator in all of this. There are just far too many coincidences and balances within our world for me to leave its creation to happenstance or blind luck.

That's just my opinion. And the reason I bring it up is because, without faith, I believe your journey to Becoming a King may require far greater resilience than I can speak to.

Personally, fulfillment and faith are massive portions to living a life that is on purpose.

One of the more common questions I get from guys is, "How does one go from where they are, in this moment, to creating a life of purpose, fulfilment, and self-worth?"

The simple answer to that is there is no straight line.

When I hike 14,000-foot peaks here in my backyard of Colorado, the terrain is so challenging and the incline so great, to go straight up the mountain would be too difficult.

Life can be that way, too. So, what have people devised as a solution to hiking extremely steep and difficult mountains? It's to use switchbacks. Essentially, you zig-zag up a mountain to decrease both the grade of incline and, thus, the difficulty. Is this the most direct way up? No, a straight line to the top would be the most direct. However, for most, such an aggressive line is reserved only for those trained and fit enough to attempt it.

It's a great metaphor for life. Because, truthfully, there is no straight line to achieving our dreams; to finding fulfilment and Becoming Kings.

Your life's experiences will always differ from those of the next guy. Which is why it is vitally important that you do not compare. What's crucial is you have a way of clarifying whether you're on the right path or not.

How that is done is by solidifying your moral compass. That way, no matter what happens, no matter what options you are given, it always points true north. It's only with this compass in place that you will know how to direct your course throughout life.

The decision to Become a King is not only to understand this concept of the Three Kingdoms, it also requires that you live by The Code of Kings.

In the next chapter, I'll explain what the code is and why it's instrumental in achieving the life of your dreams.

CHAPTER 14

The Code of Kings

"A man without ethics is a wild beast loosed upon the world."
—Albert Camus

Who Are You Committed to Being?

WITH ALL THE STUDY, research, and reading I've done over the years, I've come to notice a common thread woven through the lives of all great men.

That common thread is they all have lived by a code and a way of being.

Whether we're talking about going back thousands of years to the times of the Middle Ages or referring to current day, men who have been worthy of emulation have all lived their lives by a code.

On the flip side of the coin, there are countless men who have acquired great wealth and power only to use it to abuse others. These men are far from being Kings.

Over the last several decades, as I've fought and clawed for abundance in each Kingdom, I began to devise a code of conduct I felt good about. A code that felt genuine and not forced. This code is what I now refer to as the *Code of Kings*.

The Code of Kings is a document I refer to on a daily basis to keep me on target about who I am committed to being. The

Code of Kings document supports the transformation of who you are now into who you want to become, so you can achieve your dreams.

You don't wait until you do all the right things to get that promotion or until you have the house, the partner, or the financial success to *then* be successful. I'm sure you have heard this before, and it still stands true. You must first be the man who does the things he knows he must, so you can have the success and fulfillment you deserve. Be, do, have. Not do, have, be.

Why the Code of Kings is vitally important is because, in the world where we live (where it is increasingly easy to compare ourselves with someone on social media who is seemingly doing and achieving more than we are), it aids in keeping each of us grounded and focused on our own gifts and not those of others.

If you do not keep yourself focused on what it is you want and who you must become, it's nearly inevitable you will suffer an impending identity crisis.

Now, I'm not talking about a midlife crisis. I had my own identity crisis at age thirty, when I began to question why, exactly, I had been so adamant about fighting for a life I wasn't even happy with. What ultimately happened was the shedding of my old self in exchange for a newer version.

Since then (and over a decade later), what I have noticed is, every eighteen to twenty-four months, another shedding must happen. It becomes increasingly clear that a part of me must die for a new part of me to begin.

The interesting thing is, even though I've seen this pattern happen many times within myself, it never gets less scary or easier to shed an old layer for the new.

It's like you are on a trapeze, swinging through the air with your back to the direction you want to go. You hold the current trapeze firmly in hand, however you must heed the call to evolve as a man and leap into the unknown. Even though you're not even assured there is another empty trapeze waiting for you, you must use your momentum and leap. What you are required to do at just the right time is let go of the safety and security of the trapeze you've been holding on to, only to fly blindly through the air—all while twisting your body in hopes the new trapeze is there for you to grab ahold of.

This process is imperative, because you have to be willing to let go of who you have been, so you can fully step into who you must become. The process of twisting your body symbolizes that it can be extremely uncomfortable, but this is the cost of letting go of the old and reaching for the new in order to achieve your dreams.

For instance, when I was thirty years old and facing a divorce, I remember staring at a scary crossroad. Do I stay comfortable? Or do I go for my dreams?

Here's what I was considering.

To remain on the trapeze I was currently swinging on meant an $85,000-per-year job and no debt, but remaining bored and deeply unsatisfied with myself. It meant no growth, remaining insecure, wounded, indecisive, co-dependent, and settling for "good enough" in life but offered financial security.

Or I could let go and reach for the new trapeze, which would require a bigger version of me who would have to be courageous, outgoing, a leader, a risk-taker, worthy, better at handling rejection, focused, decisive, and willing to live an adventure.

The man I had become at that time in my life was plain ordinary. He was content in swinging on a trapeze that required no risk of falling, but this also demanded no growth. And the boredom was killing me.

The life you ultimately want is going to require some massive risk in order to let go of the comfortable and reach for new heights. That space between where you are right this moment and what you're being beckoned to reach for is the gap. The gap is the scary transition phase after having let go of what you came to depend on and before you reach a new sense of safety after leveling up.

It's scary as shit. Regardless, that transcendence will be required of you over and over and over throughout your life, if you hope to achieve your dreams, and become King of your Kingdoms.

The way I like to think about this is that at any given time throughout your day, there are two characters available to play.

There's *the Ordinary Man* and *the Extraordinary Man*.

The Ordinary Man is who you tolerate being. He is not you at your best. He is you at the lowest standards that you are willing to accept.

Whereas the Extraordinary Man is you when you are inspired, focused, and upholding higher standards. He is the version of you who makes you feel proud.

When I first began refining this process, I struggled. Because I felt as though both of these characters were me, depending on the day. However, what I've come to learn is that's not true.

These characters can be summoned and maintained whenever we want, as long as we're being intentional. And because I struggled sometimes to see a clear line of demarcation between the two, one of my coaches recommended I give them both names.

To the Ordinary Man (and the attributes he would express, such as the "nice guy," the people-pleaser, coward, bored, uninspired, and settler for "good enough"), I gave the name of Robert the Bruce, the character from *Braveheart*.

If you've ever seen *Braveheart*, you know who I'm talking about. If you haven't seen the movie, you must put it on your "to watch next" list. Robert the Bruce was a man who had good intentions, though his need to please his father and play politics made for a tumultuous experience.

And that's how I see myself whenever I fall into bad habits of attempting to make people happy. Whenever I'm acting as "Robert the Bruce" in my life, I'm acting vanilla and as a puppy dog.

Compare that to the Extraordinary Man, who acts with purpose, passion, and determination in his life. So, no matter what appears in his way, it doesn't stop him from doing what needs to be done.

He's a man who knows, when he shows up in his full power, he inspires and gives permission to others to do the same. He's not vanilla; he's a fucking *lion*! I decided to name this character "King Leonidas," from the movie *300*.

To be clear, when I'm owning my "King Leonidas" energy, it's not as if I'm emotionally disconnected and don't care what other people think. Rather, I remain compassionate, while I act in alignment with where my heart guides me. I stay true to me and don't let the opinions of others persuade me from what I want.

According to Wikipedia:

> *King Leonidas was an ancient Greek king from the city-state of Sparta. He was born sometime around 530-540 BCE into a royal household and became king around 490 BCE. He was tasked with leading a relatively small Greek force to hold the line against a much larger Persian force led by Xerxes at Thermopylae in 480 BCE.*

When I step into my King Leonidas persona, I don't care if life is throwing its version of an overwhelming "larger Persian force" against me. I stand strong and courageous against whatever comes my way. If life was easy and if the enemy of self-doubt was easily defeated, there'd be no need for courage.

I recommend you do this exercise as well. For me, Robert the Bruce and King Leonidas remind me of the qualities and energy I must embody when I read through my Code of Kings.

Now it's your turn. I want you to take a piece of paper, and write a line down the middle. On one side, write down all the ways you show up when you're feeling down, insecure, and hopeless. On the other side of the line, write how you feel when you're focused, confident, and excited for the future. Lastly, come up with two names for each persona, and then share this exercise with a couple of your closest buddies, so they can support you out of your "ordinary man" and into your "extraordinary man."

Over the years, I've created more in-depth processes for getting crystal-clear about who I had been and who I was committed to being. This process of letting go of who I had been—letting that man die, while stepping into the man I knew I must become—became the foundation for the Code of Kings.

The Code of Kings is more than a simple process. It's a guiding force for your life. When you take the time to refine what you stand for, who you're committed to being, there is no army large enough, no enemy powerful enough to dissuade you from Becoming King of the life you desire.

So, let's get to it. The very first step in creating your Code of Kings is you must first take stock of who you have been.

First, we'll do an exercise to establish some foundation for the next part of the process. So, grab yourself a journal, flip over that piece of paper you were just using, or open a Word document on your computer. Personally, I recommend you do this the old-fashioned way with pen and paper, however it's up to you. Once you have that, answer this first question...

* How would you describe who you have been, in three sentences or less?

I'll use myself as an example, to help you through this process. So, what I did first was get brutally honest with who I was and how I acted, when I was being Robert the Bruce. This is what I wrote:

> *I see myself as having amazing potential to contribute positively to the world. Even so, I feel scared, because I fear I won't be able to uphold what would be demanded of me on a daily basis. I'm scared I don't have enough motivation, drive, and strength within me to pull it off, over the long haul. I'm afraid of being just ordinary and lost in the masses of men who die with so much potential that is never tapped into.*

Second question...
- ✶ What part of the country or world are you choosing to live in? How much money do you earn? How much do you have saved? And how much debt do you owe?

This is an essential question, because it requires you to look at the hard numbers of your financials. When it comes to your standard of life, seeing the cold, hard facts is a tough pill to swallow. Still, it's absolutely necessary to no longer bury your head in the sand. You must know where you stand now, with your standard of life. And do not allow yourself to give "rough ballpark" numbers. Raise your standard and demand excellence in everything you do. Log into your financial accounts and get real hard numbers.

Next question...
- ✶ What's your current weight? How well do you currently take care of yourself? And how do you present yourself to the world?

I then looked at my good and bad habits.
- ✶ What are your good and bad habits? What are your healthy and unhealthy routines?

Many years ago, going through this process for the first time, here's what I discovered for myself...

Good Habits: I was constantly learning new things. Curious about why people do what they do. I took great care of my health. I poured my gifts into people. I had incredible friendships, and I nurtured them consistently. So far, so good. But there was another side of the coin.

Bad Habits: I cracked my knuckles and joints. I believed my shitty beliefs about not being good enough. I judged myself harshly. I often spent money as soon as I made it. I believed I was a great "second in charge," just not a true leader. I had a bad habit of watching Netflix in bed for a couple hours every night, and then shaming myself in the morning, when I'd wake up exhausted.

Why was looking at my habits worthwhile? I often tell the men I work with, "Show me your habits, and I'll show you your results." The fact is, we are what we repeatedly do.

* What are your top-five strengths and weaknesses?

Look at the negative thoughts that routinely pop into your mind on a consistent basis. Notice if there are any bad habits of past negative events that would play out in your mind.

I'd even recommend you dive into your childhood memories, to pull out any highlights and lowlights. Not surprisingly, your lowlights will likely tie directly into those things you find yourself being worried about now, as an adult.

The blocks that are keeping you from stepping into your full personal power and achieving your dreams will then come more fully into view.

As you begin to chip away at whatever you're angry about in others (and, more importantly, in yourself), it's important to look at the stories of blame you have created.

I want you to look at what activities excite and breathe life into you versus what absolutely sucks the life from you. The key is to begin doubling down on your gifts, while simultaneously creating leverage, trading for, and outsourcing to others the things you hate doing.

(Sidebar: I recommend reading *The 4-Hour Work Week* by Tim Ferris, if you want some creative insight as it relates to outsourcing and working smarter vs. harder.)

What you will realize is, when you are in resistance to something that is not a gift or strength of yours, you make it 100 times more complex.

Albert Einstein once said, "Genius is making complex ideas simple, not making simple ideas complex."

In life, we as human beings make things a lot more complicated than they need to be. For instance, countless clients of mine have told me they want to start a new business. And their next thought is, "I should put together a business plan."

Usually, what follows is, "And while I'm at it, I should probably get an online presence. So, I'll need a catchy website URL, a nice new website, a logo, business email address, business mailing address, business cards..." In other words, all the things you can think of *before* you even go out to the market to see if your business is viable.

Why do people do this? Because they're scared.

If you relate to any of this, I get it. The truth is, your brain will do whatever it can to ensure your safety by triggering your fight-or-flight behavior. Essentially, avoiding anything that could result in pain.

However, what does a healthy body require? Resistance. Stress. Muscles only grow when they have resistance thrust upon them. Without stressing our bodies, we will not grow stronger. This is precisely why it is called "resistance training." Pushing through resistance to build muscle is what results in being physically fit.

The same principle holds true for your brain, your relationships, your work, etc. What does a healthy relationship require? Staying in the fight when everything in your body says to run, to walk away, to give up. And what does a healthy career require? Risk, sacrifice, stepping into the unknown—a.k.a. pain.

So, as you can see, our brains are not hardwired for success. They're hardwired for longevity of the species. As you continue reading through this book and doing the work, your Code of Kings document will take on more and more life.

One of the most important stances you must take in Becoming a King is not only choosing to stay in the ring when the fight gets difficult; it's adopting an "above the line" mentality.

Not sure what I mean? Check this out...

CHAPTER 15

Playing Life Above or Below the Line

"Healthy habits are learned in the same way as unhealthy ones—through practice."

—Wayne Dyer

THE FIRST QUESTION you must ask yourself is, "Where am I?" Meaning, this game of life can be the most fun you've ever had, or it can be an absolute misery.

The other day, I had an interaction over text message with a buddy who cautioned me not to get brainwashed by a group of people he perceived were wrong in their opinions. I, on the other hand, wasn't attempting to take a particular stance other than one of being compassionate and empathetic to the pain these people had endured.

He went on to tell me how he was right and they were wrong. He was extremely combative and seemed eager to get into a debate.

My response was I wasn't interested in having a conversation where his sole purpose for having it was to assert his rightness. I told him he was entitled to his opinion. However, I insisted I was only interested in discussing topics of politics, race, social injustice, etc. with people who were open-minded and curious.

His response: "Oh, so you don't want to debate, because you know I'm right and you'd lose?"

What I did instead of taking the bait was to ask him how he was doing. Like how was he *really* doing? "Hey man, how're you doing? Are you doing okay? You seem angry, pissed, and looking to fight. Everything going okay in life?"

Not surprisingly, he began to open up. He said he wasn't happy with his job whatsoever. It was boring as fuck, his relationship with his wife was stagnant, and he had completely let his physical health deteriorate.

His responses didn't surprise me. I've noticed I'm only criticized by people who aren't happy with themselves. They're unclear with the direction they're going in life, and, out of that frustration, they distract themselves from their own pain by taking it out on others.

So, this is where you get to ask yourself, where are you right now in playing this game of life? Are you above or below the line?

Below the line is whenever you find yourself being closed off, defensive, and committed to being right.

Whereas being above the line is whenever you find yourself open-minded, curious, and committed to leveling up in life wherever possible.

When you're playing below the line, you often carry certain world beliefs, such as feeling there is not enough time, money, happiness, energy, or space in the world. It's a scarcity mindset. There's often a story you have created about the way things work, and your instinct is to find evidence to back up how right you feel about it.

The longer you stay below the line, the more convicted your opinion gets that there are threats to your well-being that keep you down. It becomes easy to find fault and blame others for your misfortune. You may find yourself in an endless story of overwhelm, where you justify and rationalize the evidence that asserts your ability to be right; to reinforce that you've been taken advantage of, so whoever did that has "won" while you've "lost."

Compare this to when you're playing above the line. From this place, your focus is more on growth, contribution, and learning.

Playing above the line often results in your curiosity of understanding other people's opinions and viewpoints. You will find yourself being willing to question your own beliefs by listening deeply and speaking in a way that isn't argumentative.

Someone who plays below the line often feels their life is "hard work," while the person who lives above the line feels like their life is "play," even if there are a lot of challenges.

When you're below the line, you're living a life of mere survival. A life where you often feel deeply alone. There's not a lot of creativity, receptivity, or forward thinking. In fact, people who play below the line are often either living through their past, or they're worried about what the future may bring. In either case, both keep them from achieving the goal of being present in the moment.

Put even more simply, being below the line is when someone behaves by blaming others, tearing down, denying, and making excuses. Whereas being above the line is when someone behaves by building others up, taking ownership and responsibility of their actions, and being accountable by following through.

Continue working in your Code of Kings document by answering these questions...

- ★ When you are playing "below the line," what does that look like in your life? How do you behave? What are common thoughts that go through your head?

* When you are playing "above the line," what does that look like in your life? How different do you feel when you remain empowered? How is your behavior different than when you're below the line? What are things you focus on that keep your thoughts elevated?

When you play above the line, you remain in control of your thoughts, feelings, and actions. When we play below the line, we fall out of integrity with our word and we become a victim. The biggest part of the Code of Kings in your development of Becoming a King is that of being in integrity with your word.

Let's take a closer look at what that means.

CHAPTER 16

Being a Man of your Word

"If you tell me you're going to do something, I remember. If you don't do it, I remember. We can still be cool, but your words will mean less."

—Unknown

I'M CURIOUS. How often do you lie? Would you call yourself a liar?

I ask because, for many men, myself included, when I first was asked this question, I said, "I'm absolutely not a liar."

However, the more I dug, the more it became increasingly clear that I lie to myself frequently.

Have you ever told someone you would be coming to their party or event and then bailed last minute, because you were tired?

Have you ever said you'd take care of something and then forgotten to follow through?

Yes, we're all human. Not a single one of us is perfect. However, I want you to take a closer look.

How often have you said you'll "try to make it" to a party, although you have no intention of going?

How often have you said you'll "be in touch," when you know full well you won't be?

How often have you set a time and then run late?

"C'mon Johnny," you might be thinking. "Now you're being unrealistic. Everyone is late from time to time."

Hold on—before you go into justification mode, hear me out.

I took a four-day course years ago at a hotel in Los Angeles, where a specific lesson was drilled into my head. It kicked off with the instructor giving a two-hour lecture. And just prior to giving us our first ten-minute break, he explained how it was going to work.

"We're going to take a ten-minute break," he said. "With three minutes remaining, a song will be played that is three minutes in length. When the song ends, you must be sitting in your seat, ready for our next section. Is that clear? Please stand if you are in agreement?"

Before we left, the instructor played the song in its entirety, so we all knew what it sounded like as it neared the end of the music. With all of our consent, off we went on our ten-minute break.

As the song was finishing, people were running in the door, throwing things into their bags, turning off cell phones, all sorts of craziness. And would you believe it, when the music finished, there were still a few people who hadn't yet gotten into their seat?

Little did I know, a shit storm was about to rain down on us all.

The instructor asked for everyone who had yet to sit down in their seat by the end of the music to please stand. There were three of them. And yet, only two of them stood.

Not surprisingly, he went at the man who didn't stand.

"Sir, what's your name?"

"Jeff."

"Jeff, please stand. Now, were you or weren't you in your seat prior to the ending of the music?"

"No, I was in my seat," he said confidently.

Asking all of us, the instructor said, "By a show of hands, who saw that Jeff was not in his seat by the time the music ended?"

We all raised our hands.

"So, Jeff, are you deliberately lying to us and to yourself? Or is there something else going on here?"

Long story short, it soon became a twenty-minute intervention. Each person who had been late sat uncomfortably in the hot seat as the instructor asked them how this kind of behavior not only showed up in this hotel ballroom, but also showed up in every other aspect of their lives.

Each person had an excuse, a rationalization, or justification as to why they were late in sitting their ass down in time. They had a great story about why they were right and worthy of having different standards than what we had all agreed to at the beginning of the ten-minute break.

So, I ask *you*, reader of this book, how often are you breaking your word, if even just to yourself?

You tell yourself you're going to work out today, you're going to get out of bed early, you're going to get home from work earlier, whatever the case may be. And yet, you still allow life to happen to you instead of being in integrity with what you say you're going to do.

Are you perpetually late? If you left fifteen minutes earlier than anticipated, would you have had to worry or be stressed, if you ran into traffic?

"Being your word" means taking responsibility for your thoughts, choices, and actions. I'm talking about the small *and* big things in life.

If you are committed to becoming a King of your human experience, there is no way you can achieve this other than by being your word. As men, our integrity is all we will ever really have. The material things, like health, relationships, jobs—everything apart from your own thoughts and behaviors—are fleeting. To Become Kings, you must be impeccable with your word.

If you say you're going to do something, you do it.

If you don't want to do something, you vocalize that, as well.

If you give your word and something out of your control comes up that will prevent you from being your word, then you openly renegotiate and discuss a win/win alternative. Most men struggle with this concept, because it's not easy.

Truth is, each and every time you give your word and then you break it, you are casting a vote against the man you desire to be.

By casting your vote, you cultivate to yourself and to others a culture of what you will tolerate by how you live, move, and breathe. By being the man you desire to be, you have the power to positively impact your environment and those you surround yourself with.

Continuing the work in your journal, I want you to dig deep and check in with what your heart truly desires. Too many men operate from "to-do" lists rather from what means most to them, and unfortunately there are no feelings within traditional "to-do" lists. Rather, the fact remains that men who are successful focus on their outcome and *not* on everything they have to accomplish in the achievement of a goal. They connect with the feeling of having achieved what they really want. So, answer this next question within your Code of Kings document...

* What is it that you *really* want? What is the ultimate outcome you desire?

* Why is it you want this outcome? What are your reasons for desiring it? What will achieving it give you?

* Now, being clear on what and why you want it, what are the things you can foresee needing to do in order to achieve your ultimate outcome? Write out as many specifics as possible.

Awesome, brother. Great work with those. Now, whether you're feeling a sense of clarity after completing those questions or not, don't give up on them. I recommend you continually ask yourself, "What is it that I *really* want out of this project, conversation, interaction, etc.?" Always come back to getting clarity on what it is you want, why you want it, and the "how" to achieve it often comes shortly thereafter.

Reclaiming Your Time

The next section of your Code of Kings document is to begin thinking about your life from the standpoint of Being a King and experiencing abundance and freedom. Please answer these next series of questions as thoughtfully as possible:

* If you had a couple extra hours a day that were just for you, what's something you'd love to experience, learn, or achieve?

* If you truly had more time in your day and week, how would you choose to spend it?

Now, I want you to make a list of everything you do that rob you of your time.

* What are activities or behaviors that don't really need to be done or that you do just because you're stalling, unclear about what would be time better spent? Write down a list of as many things you can think of that don't

have much purpose and yet you find yourself doing anyway.

Men who know what they want, know why they want it, and are in integrity with their word are the movers and shakers of the world. They are those people who achieve much while also living fulfilled lives, because they are connected to the greater sense of purpose behind everything they do. They are intentional, focused, and self-aware.

Not surprisingly, these Kings have tremendous positive impacts on those they interact with and in the world. They create what I call a Kingdom Culture that surrounds them. They don't allow themselves to be encircled by people who bring them down or who don't believe in what they believe. The Kingdom Culture first starts with how they treat and respect themselves. Then it grows to impact their loved ones, their significant other, their children, their closest friends, and family.

A King does not settle for toxicity in his relationships. If there is dysfunction, he faces it head on and works it through. How he shows up in his personal life is congruent with how he shows up in his business life. Not surprisingly, a King creates a Kingdom Culture of love, personal power, and integrity everywhere he goes.

If you tell me you're going to do something, I remember. If you don't do it, I remember. We can still be cool, but your words will mean less.

CHAPTER 17

Building a Kingdom Culture

"At some point you have to toss aside the things and people that don't work and just build your empire."

— Travis Simmons

IT'S INTERESTING to note, among the companies that rank as the most desired places to work, most employees attribute this quality to their workplace culture.

So, what is it that's so important about the culture and work environment?

It's my feeling, in a world where we have so many ways to connect, for many it's superficial. It's likely based more on people seeking significance and a boost to their fragile self-worth than it is focused on genuine connection and value added.

Truth is, people are feeling extremely lonely at this time in human history.

Think about it in terms of how Apple operates. When you walk into an Apple store, there is a clear difference in how their stores make you feel, how they approach their customer service experience, and the way their employees behave and respond. Do you think Apple's corporate culture is coincidence? Or that it evolved by happenstance? Of course not.

Not surprisingly, some of the relationships and families of friends I admire most are just as intentional as Apple is.

These friends have a written mission and list of values their entire family has agreed to uphold, parents and children alike.

During my interview of Dr. Robert Glover, author of *No More Mr. Nice Guy*, he recommended men "begin by building a tribe and start opening up to them."

Very few men have a tribe, a group of men who are all committed to a culture by which they live. As men who sit at the throne of their lives, every day we have the choice to intentionally pursue a life of abundance or a life of mediocrity.

When you decide you're going to live your life with the highest standards of excellence for yourself, then you decide to create a Kingdom Culture that has the power to change your life, the lives of those you love, and, thus, the world.

Changing the world becomes the by-product of showing up as a man on purpose. Every room you walk into, every person you interact with, every family meal you sit down at, you broadcast your Kingdom Culture as a part of you. Kingdom Culture is an intentional way of behaving, responding, walking, and talking.

Don't get me wrong—the pursuit of creating this type of culture is not for the faint of heart.

Being a representative of Kingdom Culture is so important and not just when things are easy. It's even more important on the days that are especially difficult. And this is precisely why you must have the humility to lean on your fellow brothers.

I heard a talk recently given at Red Rocks Church here in Denver, Colorado, by Pastor Shawn Johnson that really resonated with me. During it, he spoke of the analogy of the thermometer and the thermostat. All a thermometer can do is detect and describe the current temperature. It reacts to whatever the temperature is around it. Whereas a thermostat has the ability to regulate the temperature of any room it's connected to.

That's what we get to do as Kings. As representatives of the Kingdom Culture, we elevate the culture around us by tapping into the truth within each of us. So, how then do you cultivate a Kingdom Culture within you and within those around you?

Building your Kingdom Culture requires several things:

1. The humility to be in service to something greater than yourself.

    When done correctly, living in service to others will change you from the inside out. You will live with an inner strength, an inner confidence, such that people will notice how the energy shifts around them. Because you'll be bringing the elevated standards that accompany a Kingdom Culture with you everywhere you go.

2. The awareness to be wherever your feet are.

    Or, said a different way, you are whole and present to the moment. Your only focus is on the here and now and what's in front of you. You're not lost in comparison to others or to where you think you should be. You are simultaneously aware of your wholeness in this moment and of the desire to expand, going forward.

3. You stay grounded mentally and emotionally.

    As your Kingdom grows in influence, there will come increasing opposition from those who will want to see it fall. Being King doesn't mean you don't have bad days. It just means you keep things in perspective.

My grandfather, Jack Miner (who was lovingly known as Daddo in our family), often reminded me of something important. Specifically, if whatever was bothering me wouldn't matter in a month, then I shouldn't worry about it.

Do not become a victim of worrying over, or gossiping about, the here and now to the point where you cannot focus on your vision of the future.

Bestselling author Alison Armstrong said in an interview on my podcast, "Part of being a King is defining yourself."

From this place of remaining humble by serving a greater good, staying present, and remaining emotionally grounded, your Kingdom Culture will have a profoundly positive impact upon the world. And God knows, we need that type of energy more than ever.

When you're on autopilot, you allow yourself to adopt whatever culture is present in the moment. Instead of maintaining a high standard, you run the risk of just learning to adapt, in order to stay comfortable.

The "Oardinary Man" lives by a culture of fear, scarcity, and isolation. He's the thermometer. The "Extraordinary Man" sets the temperature by raising his standards around what he's no longer willing to settle for. He represents the thermostat.

You and I are not going to change the world by being led by our egos and taking offense to the opinions of others. We're also not going to change the world by yelling louder that our opinions are right and attempting to silence the opinions of others. And we're certainly not going to change the world by fighting for who is the bigger victim.

By building a Kingdom Culture, we're going to change the world by first changing ourselves. And we're going to do it by being the best at forgiveness; especially, loving those who have differing opinions than our own.

Let me state for the record, however: it's natural human behavior to be scared of, and to protect yourself from, things you don't know or understand. And because of this, we often build an invisible wall of beliefs meant to keep us safe and out of harm's way.

We create beliefs about people, about life, and how the world works.

For most ordinary people, they never question the validity of those beliefs. Instead, they spend a lifetime fortifying and strengthening those invisible walls to maintain their personal safety, or so they believe.

However, the solution to a life of fulfillment, abundance, and the life of a King is counterintuitive to natural human behavior. Alternatively, you've got to realize that progress will never be achieved unless you're willing to break down your invisible wall. And you do that by connecting with people who don't look like you, who don't live like you, and who don't believe what you believe.

That's what it looks like to create a Kingdom Culture.

Somehow, as men, we've come to think that insulting, shaming, and punishing others is going to be our biggest weapon for change. But yet, what will ultimately succeed is quite the opposite.

Let me make one last distinction, though. By stating that building a Kingdom Culture of service, awareness, and humility is the path to healing, I'm not telling you to lose your fervor for being a warrior at heart. I'm asking you to remain warriors for change, for healing, elevating thought, and for creating win/win scenarios in all your dealings.

Love in action never loses its zeal. Do not fall victim to becoming passive. Anyone can argue on social media or gossip about those they disagree with behind their backs. But it takes real strength, courage, and personal power of restraint to create progress through love.

So, I encourage you to gather with those who are committed to living the Kingdom Culture and to going out into the world to raise the standards of how men are viewed and respected.

CHAPTER 18

The Game

"Just play. Have fun. Enjoy the game."
—Michael Jordan

THIS IS THE GAME. The game of life. It's a game where you battle against the smaller version of you and your true capacity.

The Ordinary Man settles for "good enough," and he does not stand in integrity with his word. With each occurrence of breaking his word, he chips away at his self-esteem. With each vote against himself, he loathes himself a little more.

Going back to the metaphor of building your Kingdom, what is required of any King is the need for a castle. This is a big part of solidifying your Inner Kingdom: creating boundaries where this metaphorical castle is erected to provide you with protection from the outside.

However, as strong as your castle may be, if there is to be even one traitor within, an impostor posing as an ally, there can be no security.

This impostor, this traitor within, is the Ordinary Man we spoke of previously. He's an enemy whose sole directive is to inflict damage to your self-esteem, creating a crack in the foundation of your castle.

For example... The Ordinary Man. This enemy from within finds it increasingly easy to turn to porn than to make love to his wife, especially when things have been strained, because he's worried his advances will be rejected.

It's far easier for the Ordinary Man to turn on a device to numb himself than it is to pick up the phone and reconcile with a long-term friend with whom he's fallen out of rapport.

It's much easier for the Ordinary Man to spend long hours engrossed in work that "pays the bills" than it is to go home early enough to cheer on his teenage son at his baseball game.

The battle you are waging within is that of the Ordinary Man vs. the Extraordinary Man.

The Extraordinary Man does *not* settle, and he is willing to do whatever it takes to honor his word. He is committed to being a man worthy of emulation by future generations.

How do you become him?

You must choose to be him each and every time the Ordinary Man appears.

When you are tempted to tuck tail and run, because you don't like confrontation or the path ahead seems difficult, this is when you must walk forward into the battle.

In those moments when you would rather remain the "pleaser" by keeping your mouth shut, you must speak your truth. The truth of what your needs are in the moment.

If you want to increase your masculine strength, you must be willing to courageously step into the darkness of your own soul to reconcile whatever is wounded within.

This is *not* about you being unworthy, not good enough, or a fuck-up. That is the biggest lie I have ever heard. Instead, this is *all* about you committing your full heart to winning this battle of tug o' war between being ordinary and being extraordinary.

Because, honestly, that is what this life is all about. It's about being a man who is worthy of your son's or daughter's emulation.

I often say your life can either be a warning of what *not* to become or an example of what's possible.

Choose the latter.

The only way we can make this world a better place, as cliché as that is, is by becoming our best versions of ourselves. Each and every day.

If not, then what's the fucking point of this human experience? To make lots of money and acquire a ton of shit you don't get to take with you?

Fuck that.

My desire, whenever my end of days arrives, is to be able to look back upon my life and clearly and confidently say I lived my life with purpose, integrity, and love.

I want future generations, whether they are my own kin or not, to have a leg up on where I was at their age. Likewise, I want you to use your life to act as a springboard for future generations, so they too can live lives of passion, purpose, and promise. That's the best way our legacies can be remembered, when you and I are gone.

So? What do *you* want to be remembered for?

That you worked a lot and were never present? Or, if you were there, that you were always depressed, anxious, or numb? Unable to connect emotionally with those who love you the most? Emotionally shut down, wounded, short tempered, bitter, resentful, abusive?

Brother, that's not the way.

The way of Becoming Kings is by living your life by your own Code of Kings.

It is not my place to tell you how you should live your life. I can offer guidance and support, sure. However, dictating it is not my place. The Code of Kings is a framework to help you define what it means for *you* to be a man of your word, one who is proud of who you have become.

A big part of "Becoming Kings" is to always be living your life intentionally rather than unintentionally. It's to be living your life according to *your* design, not anyone else's. So, as we dig into this concept, my question for you is this...

What is Success?

When will you determine that you've become successful?

Perhaps you already have. Or perhaps there's a part of you that believes it's unachievable.

The way I see it, success is *not* a destination. Rather, it's a state of mind.

I remember, nearly ten years ago, I was watching an interview with "The Lifestyle King"—a.k.a. real-estate guru Dean Jackson. He was talking about success and the list he had made to remind himself of when he was "being" successful.

Did you catch that key word he used?

It wasn't a list to measure *when* he "achieved" success. It was a list of when he knew he was "being" successful. Right now. At this moment. That subtle difference made a massive mindset shift for me, because I had always put "success" out there as an elusive carrot I was forever chasing. A goal, rather than a process.

However, Dean reframed the concept to the point where I realized I could achieve "being successful" today, in this moment. My mind was blown.

He went on to share his list which went like this...

I Know I'm Being Successful When:

1. I can wake up every day and ask, "What would I like to do today?"
2. My passive revenue exceeds my lifestyle needs.
3. I can live anywhere in the world I choose.
4. I'm working on projects that excite me and allow me to do my best work.
5. I can disappear for several months with no effect on my income.
6. There are no whiny people in my life.
7. I wear my watch for curiosity only.
8. I have no time obligations or deadlines.
9. I wear whatever I want all the time.
10. I can quit anytime.

With this list, Dean was able to stay centered as he looked at business decisions and other opportunities that came up in his life.

Dean also often asks if a particular decision will move him more in alignment with his top-ten list or further away.

So, success is nothing to achieve. Instead, it's something you attract. It is attracted by becoming an attractive person to the marketplace. Success is not something you pursue. It's a completely different mindset.

Once you get clear about what it is you want, the key is to become more attractive to people in that marketplace.

Are you seeking love? How are you going to become a more attractive man to the partner you want to be with?

Are you seeking more passion and love in your current relationship? In what ways are you working to become more passionate and loving?

Are you seeking greater impact and income? Then, in what ways are you making yourself more attractive and valuable to *that* marketplace?

At the end of the day, what's important is you are clear with who you are and what you stand for.

A lot of men think, to become more successful, they need to pursue more skills and education (i.e., knowledge).

Interestingly enough, a research study (conducted by Harvard University, the Carnegie Foundation, and Stanford Research Center over a thirty-year period) took a look at what factors made the biggest difference amongst their alumni. What were the variables between those who found themselves in more prestigious, better-paying jobs, and other graduates who had the same education?

What they took thirty years to determine, I'd like to illustrate for you in the next sixty seconds.

Harvard Study Exercise

- First, I want you to envision someone you admire and consider successful. A person you would love to spend time with; someone who you would die to have mentor you.
- Now, on a piece of paper, I want you to list out all the attributes you admire that makes this person seem successful to you. What makes them a leader, someone you admire?
- Go ahead and write down all your answers.

Now—for the purposes of this experiment—I'm going to imagine you wrote down some or all of the same things that come to mind when I do the same exercise. When I think of someone who is successful, I think of them as a leader.

Determined, persistent. Someone of integrity who is driven. They have a clear vision, they're powerful, balanced, and healthy. They never quit, they have high standards for themselves, they have great relationships, they're good with money, they communicate well, they're focused, and they demand respect. This person is humble, self-aware, articulate, passionate, intelligent, empathetic, authentic, honest, and, well—the list goes on and on.

I have a sneaky feeling your list is similar to mine.

What the study did next was to look at the three key areas most likely to determine someone's success in life:

✓ An individual's knowledge
✓ Skills and
✓ Attitude

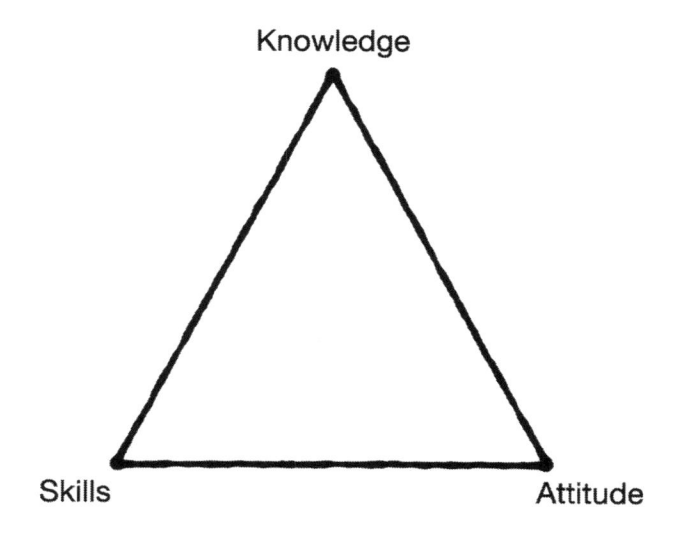

```
         Knowledge
            /\
           /  \
          /    \
         /      \
        /        \
       /          \
      /_____\
   Skills         Attitude
```

They took a look at lists like yours and mine. And the study ultimately concluded that eighty-five percent of job success comes from having well-developed people skills and attitude, (soft skills) and only fifteen percent of job success comes from technical skills and knowledge (hard skills).

What I love about this study is it begins to shed light on an important question. Specifically: what makes the biggest difference in people, in their performance, and in their final results in life?

Is it usually dependent upon skill? Is it that they're *really* knowledgeable?

I would put money on the fact you've met or read a story of someone with unbelievable natural skill who got wiped out by an athlete, a person, or a business individual who clearly had *less* skill.

And how is this?

Any time anyone outperforms someone else with greater skill, it is because of their ability to maximize.

I hate to break it to you, brother. It's not how many degrees you have or how many letters you have behind your name. What will make you a leader is when you have a higher expectation. Not of other people, but of yourself.

So, do you want to know what will take you to the highest level, to become a King of each area of your life? And not temporarily, but permanently?

You must raise your standards.

Let me ask you a few questions...

If you get into a groove, and you begin to hit the gym on a routine basis, how long will you remain fit and healthy?

If you have taken your business to the next level, because you're doing all the right things, how long will you have to do those things, if you want your business to continue to thrive?

If you decide you're going to rekindle your relationship, and you go back to doing all the things you did at the beginning that created excitement, romance, and love, how long will you need to do those things, to maintain a fulfilling connection with your significant other?

I think you get my point.

If you want to live like a King, this book cannot be what I refer to as just a "Jacuzzi Moment."

That's when something feels really good in the moment, but as soon as you close the book or you turn off the podcast, those feelings prove fleeting.

The reality is, if change is going to be lasting, then the things you've learned from this book need to become the standard for your lifestyle of becoming a King. Not something you only do for a period of time.

To truly level up your life, you've got to raise your standards!

CHAPTER 19

The Foundation

"The quality of a leader is reflected in the standards they set for themselves."

—Ray Kroc

Creating a Life Plan

SO, WHEN I SAY you've got to raise your standards, what exactly do I mean?

Have you ever heard the saying, "Good is the enemy of great"?

It means everything you've been putting off by saying, "I know I should..." needs to become something about which you say, "I'm glad I am..." This could include working out more, eating better, creating more clarity in your work, scheduling more date nights, spending more time with your kids, cutting back on your spending, paying off your debt, losing weight, and so on. Whatever it is you tell yourself you "should" do, they have to become "musts."

At the end of the day, the difference in people's lives, their lifestyles, and their results is the difference in their "shoulds" vs. their "musts."

For instance, brother: the current state of your body and appearance is a direct reflection of your standards for physical health. We get what we are willing to tolerate in life.

We are certainly not a reflection of our hopes and desires. We don't get our goals just because we desire them.

What we get in life is tied to what our musts are, our standards, and who we are committed to becoming, all of which show up in our daily rituals.

Think about it. Your "shoulds" are those things you do only when they're convenient, easy to attain, and don't create any discomfort.

I'm sure you've also had times in your life when you've hit an emotional threshold and said, "Enough is enough. This *must* change."

When you've gotten to this point, what have you done to change? Anything it takes, right? No matter what, you've found a way to get it done.

That's the main difference in peoples' lives: what their shoulds are vs. what their musts are (i.e., what their standards are).

Another key aspect to becoming a King, living a wealthy life of both achievement *and* fulfillment, is dependent upon who you surround yourself with.

As the saying goes, "Who you spend your time with is who you become."

We are the sum total of the five people we spend the most time with. Think about it: if everyone around you lives to eat rather than eats to live, chances are high you won't maintain a healthy body. If everyone around you is constantly tired, after a while (even if you have high energy), gradually and subconsciously, you lower your own standards just a little.

And that little bit is that old metaphor we touched on previously: if you take a frog and put it in boiling water, what's it going to do? It's going to jump right out. But if you put a frog in water and turn up the heat slowly? Over time, it'll boil to death.

That's most people's lives, isn't it?

And it's true because most people forget that who they spend the most time with is who they become.

This is precisely why I choose to work out either in a group setting or with a motivated training buddy at the gym. During the coronavirus pandemic, I worked out by myself at home for months. And it took some serious effort to raise my standards to push as hard as I do when I'm in a group class or at the gym around other people who are also pushing hard.

Personally, I feed off the energy of people. I'm an extrovert, so working out at home became increasingly difficult. However, what I had to do was create a scenario in my head. One where I was jailed at home for three months, and I was determined to come out of it fitter, healthier, and with greater clarity for my life.

It was during the coronavirus pandemic that I began writing this book.

So, whether you're working out, playing a sport, or sharing time with someone who's playing at a higher level than you in life, this is what it comes down to. If you want to change your life, you must raise your standards.

And if you want to *dramatically* increase your standards, put yourself around those who are playing the game at a much higher level than you. That is what I have done, and it's changed my life immensely.

The Power of Mentorship

Even the greatest athletes of all time have always had coaches and trainers, because they're committed to constantly improving.

If something is wrong with your car, would you go to a dentist? Of course not. You'd go to a mechanic.

If you're struggling with your relationship, are you going to hire an accountant? No way.

A professional personal trainer, financial planner, accountability coach, or mechanic brings a level of specialized experience and knowledge of their field to bear on your situation. A level of expertise that allows them to anticipate potential moves in advance, far earlier than when the general public might.

When "the Great One," Wayne Gretzky, was asked what made him one of the best hockey players of all time—even though he wasn't the fastest, strongest, or most talented—what was his reply?

"Most people skate to where the puck is. I skate to where the puck is going."

There is so much wisdom in that statement.

You can do the same thing. However, it requires you to get clear about where you want to go. If the puck represents the man you are to become, then you need to move in the direction of where the puck is going.

Selecting the right mentor to take you and your mindset to the next level is one of the biggest decisions you have the opportunity to make. Truth be told, mentors and coaches are so vital to your journey because good ones will be able to see your scotomas—a.k.a. your blind spots.

They will bring your attention to things you cannot see that are holding you back, like your limiting beliefs.

And what are those? Let's get into that.

Change your Limiting Beliefs

Let me ask you, who has limiting beliefs?

That's a trick question, because everyone does.

The challenge is that most of yours are not visible at first glance. So, you've got to become aware enough to destroy them.

As the late automotive mogul Henry Ford once said, "Whether you think you can or you can't, either way you are right."

Whatever you're certain about, you'll find a way to support it. Have you noticed, if you want to find evidence to support a belief, you'll always be able to find something on the Internet to validate it?

Let's look at a very simple example of how our viewpoints confirm our beliefs.

- ➢ Whether you're sitting or standing, I want you to reach an arm up and point at something above your head. It doesn't matter whether it's the ceiling or the sky.
- ➢ Now, with your finger still pointing, begin drawing an imaginary circle around a fixed point while making sure your index finger moves in a clockwise direction.
- ➢ Next, with your hand still above your head, finger pointed, continuing to draw an imaginary circle with your finger moving clockwise, lower your hand to the point where your finger is now below your chin and you're looking down at your index finger as it points upward.
- ➢ Keep moving your hand in the same circular motion.
- ➢ Tell me now: is your hand moving clockwise or counterclockwise? Did you change the direction of your hand?

No, you did not.

However, notice, when you're looking at your hand from underneath, your finger drew a circle in a clockwise direction. And yet, when you moved your hand to below your chin, your finger was now drawing a counterclockwise circle—when nothing had changed except your perspective.

This example demonstrates the same principle as our limiting beliefs. All that is required of us is a change of perspective for our lives to be dramatically changed.

Have you ever noticed that emotionally fit men—those who are happy—only seem to get happier? While men who are depressed only seem to get more depressed?

Let's look at it another way.

Imagine it's winter. If you were caught outside without the proper clothing, tools, and equipment, how miserable might you be? Could this even be life-threatening? You bet.

Now, imagine *with* the proper clothing, tools, and equipment (and let's say a pair of skis)—how much fun could you have in the coldest of environments? You could have one of the best days of your life.

If you're prepared, with all the right tools, equipment, and mindset, no matter the circumstances you find yourself in, you can thrive in any environment.

The best way to begin is by implementing these five changes to your life:

1. Starting with your lifestyle, raise your standards—turn your "shoulds" into "musts."

2. You've got to go out and change your limiting beliefs— find anything that's limiting you and destroy it. The fastest way to destroy it is to envision the results in your mind over and over again *or* get yourself in a state of absolute certainty.

3. To get maximum results, model what works! If you don't believe you have the support to follow through, then hire someone who can support you in implementing your new "musts." If you don't believe you have the money (a.k.a. the resources), then be resourceful. Ask for a trade, or challenge yourself to find the resources.

4. Intensify and innovate by rigging the game of life in your favor. Set up your rules so it becomes very easy for you to feel fulfilled.

5. The best way to achieve this is by stepping up to give more than anyone else could possibly expect. Under-promise and over-deliver every time out.

The ultimate transformation happens when you stop attempting to get, and you instead start to give.

Whenever you're giving, you're at your best!

Giving is the secret to living!

CHAPTER 20

The Audit

"The ones who are crazy enough to think they can change the world are the ones who do."

—Steve Jobs

Keeping Score

I IMAGINE YOU'VE heard the saying, "Time is money."

Do you believe this is true? What *is* time, when you really think about it?

As I previously mentioned, time is relative to the emotions you're feeling. For instance, I'm sure you've also heard, "Time flies when you're having fun!"

Just like my perfect day on the lake with my buddies—when I'm having a blast, in an amazing conversation, and living life to the fullest, time flies by.

When I was seven years old, while riding my bike I was hit by a car. And I remember vividly how time passed as if it was in slow motion. It was trippy.

So, my point is, time really is relative to the emotions we experience.

As life goes, so goes time. Where your focus goes, your energy flows.

In working with men during the ten-plus years I've been a coach, I noticed they often gauge their time by whether they're productive or making money. They often mistake movement for achievement.

This is why becoming a master of your time is so important: because where we spend our time is what we value.

I remember an instance of this from when I was in a relationship. She asked me, "You once told me I was the most important thing in your life. And yet, when I look at how you spend your time, I feel like your work, rehabbing the house, studying for your MBA, and getting ready for your bodybuilding competition all take priority over me. I'm fourth or fifth in line, at best."

And you know what? She was right.

Within the next thirty days, I finished the house, dropped out of my MBA program and attended my competition. I needed to put my money (i.e., my time) where my mouth was and step up.

Any time your partner thinks there is something that comes between you and them—that something else takes greater priority—you're going to have issues in the relationship. I learned that the hard way.

Having said that, I also realize it's very difficult to strike a balance between everything that's important.

For you to win this game called life, you've got to become extremely clear about the areas of life that matter most to you. This is precisely why the Ordinary Man is not fit and healthy.

It is why the Ordinary Man is not in a relationship that is tremendously passionate.

This is why the Ordinary Man is not financially earning what he wants to earn.

Very few men have those things. However, there are a few that do.

There are the few men who do live as Kings, with a life that is happy, fulfilled, financially strong, physically fit, emotionally and spiritually alive, with their career or business thriving, and who are in a relationship that is a passionate love affair.

And this is precisely why I've written this book. Because I'm obsessed with finding the key distinctions between the few men who do live as Kings and the rest who settle for being ordinary.

The mere fact you're reading this book tells me you are motivated to be one of the few committed to becoming a King, versus the majority, who only talk a good game about leveling up.

So, what we want to do next is to create some *massive momentum*!

The first step is you must first get yourself into a peak physical and emotional state.

Turn on some music that pumps you up, get your body moving, say some powerful affirmations aloud, and stand as though you were invincible—as if you were 100% confident in yourself and what your life's mission is.

If that's difficult for you to step into, then imagine yourself as someone you see as extremely confident. A superhero; someone you look up to. It doesn't matter who it is, just stand as if you were them.

Good!

The next step is to increase your level of awareness. You will do this by tracking.

I typically ask my one-on-one and mastermind clients to perform a time audit for at least one day, if not for an entire week. On a spreadsheet, every thirty minutes, write down what they've been doing.

For clients who want to make more money, I have them track their spending, down to every penny, for twenty-one days.

For unhealthy clients, I have them track the food they currently ingest, prior to us changing their nutrition and exercise routines.

Tracking sounds tedious. Regardless, it works. Because it brings moment-to-moment awareness to the actions you are performing on a daily basis. It holds you accountable to the process of what requires improvement in your life, in order to level-up.

As I've learned over the years, you cannot manage something you do not measure. The better you measure something, the higher the probability you'll have to achieve your desired outcome.

You will never be able to tap into your talents, resources, and capabilities, or become the man you are proud to be until you are aware of and accountable for your actions.

Think about it: every Olympic athlete has a team of coaches who track their every move. They track their nutrition, supplementation, sleeping habits, heart rate, recovery period, and so many other factors, just so they will be able to help the athlete perform at their highest.

Once you begin the process of tracking, the next step is to get clear about what you're passionate about! Too many people decide to make a change because they're sick and tired of where they currently are. However, they don't then go on to take the time to truly decide on what it is that they want to create or what brings them true fulfillment.

When you begin to focus on the things that light you up and make you feel pumped, you'll find that what you value most will be in alignment with what keeps the fire lit inside you.

So, let's not just talk about this as theory. Let's do some of the heavy lifting.

In your Code of Kings document, write out your answers to the following questions:

* What are the things that are soul-sucking, that you hate, that draw life from you?
* What are the things you value most, that you love, that breathe life into you?
* When you're in that emotional state of being psyched, without limiting yourself, what is it that you *really* want out of life?
* What is it that really motivates you, pushes you forward, incentivizes you in life?

Now that you've gotten that work out of the way, the third step in this process of creating *massive momentum* is to follow through by making a decision to act.

The word "decide" comes from the Latin word, "*decaedere*," which means to "cut off" and to "bring to a settlement."

So, continuing that work of pen and paper, write down a couple examples of decisions you've made in life that have had a profoundly positive impact upon you.

* In what ways did that decision improve your life, and what was the tipping point that finally got you to make the decision and act?
* Thinking about your life currently, what are a couple of decisions you must make a commitment to now? And in doing so, how will they positively impact your life going forward?

The next step is to take *massive action*!

A big part of this process (not within the scope of this book, but something you can do nonetheless through my online e-courses at www.JohnnyKing.com) is to create a powerfully impactful plan. Without a plan, it'll be a lot more difficult to take thoughtful, consistent action in the direction you want your life to go.

So, once you have your dialed-in massive action plan, the last and final step is to consistently manage and strengthen it. You've got to decide if you're getting the results you want. (Remember: success is a process, not a result.) And if not, then it's time to make subtle adjustments without being too attached to "how" you're going to achieve your results.

Being attached to your vision of what you want to create is imperative.

Being unattached to how you're going to make it a reality is what brings maturity and confidence.

Be willing to take new action in ways you haven't in the past, in case what you're doing isn't getting you the results you really want. Your ego will often attempt to sabotage you in this.

When it does, pick up the phone and ask for some input from a friend. Or shoot me an email. I'd be happy to help you break through, if you feel like you've run into resistance along the way.

The truth is, there are a lot of spiritual masters who recommend dissolving one's ego precisely because it often attempts to sabotage you in its effort to protect you.

When I was interviewing the always-insightful and powerful coach, Stefanos Sifandos, I asked him if it was important to dissolve one's ego. His reply was, "Yes and...."

As he put it, "If you dissolve your ego without healing those wounded parts of yourself, it's a recipe for fucking disaster. Dissolving your ego is a very advanced practice, and there are so many processes that precede that. The ego is the way we identify with the world, and part of the ego is to protect us. So, we develop these coping strategies as we grow up, and they're invested in our ego, because it determines how we see ourselves and how we think others see us."

He went on to say you must heal those wounded parts of yourself, prior to working on dissolving your ego. So, it's great to be aware of the role your ego plays in your life and to dance with it. It can act as your greatest adversary, however. If you can work toward greater levels of integration, you can slowly detach yourself from it.

An incredible way of healing is to replace old, unhealthy habits with healthier ones. Through this process, you will gain greater confidence in yourself. The trick is it just takes time.

CHAPTER 21

Rituals and Results

"A nail is driven out by another nail; habit is overcome by habit."

—Erasmus

HABITS... THEY'RE nothing sexy, usually.

In fact, Dictionary.com defines a "habit" as: "an acquired behavior pattern regularly followed until it has become almost involuntary."

So many of our daily routines have become so habituated, we're not even aware of them. Essentially, your body becomes more adept at performing the habit than your mind does. I've heard of it referred to as "muscle memory." Habits are often automatic or unconscious thoughts, behaviors, and emotions that come as a result of a lot of repetition.

You, my friend, are the sum total of all your rituals and routines.

For someone who is fit and healthy, their habit and routine are to eat right and exercise regularly.

Someone who is *not* fit and healthy? Their routine and habit is that they don't eat right and don't exercise regularly.

Mind-blowing, right? (I say that sarcastically) Let's take this a step further. For instance, we often think of habits as things we *do*. Like brushing our teeth, taking the same route to and from the office each day, and other ways we go about our day. However, less obviously, we have just as many habits that happen in our thinking that determine our way of *being*.

Someone who is routinely sad likely has a habit of thinking about their problems on a routine basis. And those problems are wired to painful memories in the brain. Now, the interesting thing is that the brain is, in many ways, a recording of the past. So, as soon as that person begins to think of those memories that make him feel sad or depressed, he's no longer in the present.

Each time he accesses any of those painful memories connected to people, places, and time, he is allowing his habit of accessing his past to dictate his current emotional state.

As I've written earlier in this book, what you direct your focus on determines how you feel. Your focus is determined by what you think, and what you think about creates your emotional state.

The scary part of this habit is that this person will live in a loop. At that point, the pain and suffering perpetuate themselves and predictably become his experience.

So why then are habits so difficult to change?

It's because of the way our brains are built. Remember: our brains always want to protect us from pain. This is why instant gratification is so addictive. Think about it: if rather than instant gratification, you received instant *magnification* of your choices, things would be different.

What do I mean by "instant magnification"? For example, if taking one bite of that pizza put an additional eighty pounds of fat on your body, so you immediately felt short of breath, began sweating profusely, and spontaneously developed high cholesterol and type 2 diabetes..., I bet you'd think twice about whether that bite was worth it.

If taking that drink of alcohol immediately transported you to your doctor's office, where you were told your liver was failing, you'd probably think twice about taking a sip.

That's not how our brains and bodies work, though. The changes aren't that sudden. When someone who is obese dies as a result of a heart attack, it's not the most recent McDonald's binge that brought it upon them. It's the result of the countless visits over the course of a lifetime that accumulate into a state of unhealthiness.

Let's take a look at it from a different angle. There's a rule of thumb in aviation that states: each degree of being off course over a distance of sixty nautical miles results in being one nautical mile off course.

So, for instance, what if you were flying from Los Angeles to Hawaii (2,479 miles) and you were one degree off course the entire time? You'd end up nearly fifty miles off course by the time you should be landing.

Life works the same way.

A "tiny" one-percent difference in you choosing well vs. not well—choosing instant gratification vs. long-term benefits—creates a *massive* difference in the outcome of your life.

I've heard it for years: "C'mon, it's just one bite. It won't kill you. Live a little!"

Maybe. Even so, what they don't realize is that the one-percent rule is still in effect. Whether we look at positive or negative habits, they have a compounding effect one way or another.

The truth is once again in what I earlier quoted Tony Robbins as saying: "If you show me your rituals, then I'll show you your results."

Just like money that compounds over time, your small, seemingly incremental shitty habits will compound into disastrous results. That is, unless you become more aware of the long-term effects of your choices. Just making a few slight improvements to your daily rituals can have amazingly profound results upon your life.

The funny thing is, small changes in your life are sustainable. And yet, because they're not big and sexy changes, a lot of times men will discredit making them. They think, "What's the point of reading for five minutes before turning off the light for the night?" Or, "What difference will my doing twenty push-ups each morning really make?"

And conversely, to focus on implementing *huge* life-altering changes to overhaul your life is exciting. However, sustaining that level of change is extremely difficult, when it's not accomplished in bite-sized, daily upgrades.

Knowing this, I hope you're convinced that the seemingly inconsequential upgrades in your day-to-day lifestyle can—over time—become life-changers.

In college, I read a book called *Rich Dad, Poor Dad* by Robert Kiyosaki. In it, he stated, "The difference between the wealthy and the middle class is solely in how they choose to spend their spare time."

I've never forgotten that. And it's not to say I don't watch Netflix or chill out. However, after I read that? I cut out all video gaming and limited movie watching for the rest of my college experience.

And what happened? I ended up having to get more creative with having fun in college. Now, I have *so* many amazing memories, because my friends and I were out of the dorm and creating fun chaos vs. sitting in our rooms, playing *GoldenEye 007* on Nintendo 64 all day and night long.

You've got to become very aware of how tempting and slippery a slope life can be, when you fall victim to the drift a lot of men slide into during their lives.

Rather than devote intentional energy into figuring out and executing what they want out of life, these men drift through their days, waiting for lightning to strike; waiting for the big lottery win. Waiting for life to come to *them,* instead of going out and getting it!

Hate to tell you, brother—that's not the way to be the King of your life.

What's the biggest part of creating a life you can be proud of, a life of fulfillment and abundance, a life where you are the King of your Kingdoms? It's to clarify why you're committed to doing whatever is necessary in order to realize your dreams.

This is why getting a clear vision of what you want out of life is so important.

As the Good Book says, "Where there is no vision, the people perish."

Brother, you've got to get clear about what you want your life to look like. When I was first instructed to craft a clear vision of my future, that was initially really difficult for me to create out of thin air. That's why I started small, like with how I want to start my perfect day. I took a piece of paper and wrote out what my perfect day would consist of. Granted, I have a couple different versions of whether I'm living my perfect "vacation" day or my perfect "work" day. Even so, there is a lot of overlap.

As I continually update my vision, I routinely sit down to ask myself, who do I want to wake up next to? What do I want to do with my day? What type of work do I want to be contributing to? Are there children in that vision? When I start there, it's a lot easier for me to think about how my perfect day would unfold. Here's an example of my perfect day:

I envision the alarm going off at 5 a.m. I wake up next to the woman of my dreams. I waste no time starting my morning routine, before the business of life takes over for the day.

I get a great workout in (which my partner chooses to join me for or not). After that, she joins me for a steamy, sexy shower prior to our getting dressed and ready for the day. We have a few minutes to enjoy a quiet breakfast together before the kids awaken and the house comes alive.

For sixty minutes, she and I are all hands on deck, making breakfasts, getting kids dressed, finding shoes, and getting backpacks and lunches put together before we take them to school.

Then it's home by 9 a.m., when I disappear to my beautiful home office to meet with my team and crush out a ton of important yet non-urgent work for the day. I'm done with work by 3 to 4 p.m., just in time for the kids to get home from school.

Since my perfect day is a Friday, I see us all getting on our mountain bikes for a trail ride or going for a hike in the mountains with the dogs.

Then, it's home to clean up and eat dinner prior to putting the kids down to bed. Later, it's time for an evening get-together with two other couples, who show up at 8:30 to have drinks and laughs around the fire pit out back, as we catch up and gaze at the stars.

By 11:00, my wife and I are finishing the day with more romantic intimacy before sleeping soundly.

Would my day really be regimented so closely by time? No, I don't necessarily like to live by the clock. I just wanted to give you an example of how specific one could get.

And either way, when I envision that day and experience being active, the intimacy with my partner, spending quality time with our kids, doing powerfully important work, having laughs, relaxing under the stars by the fire with amazing friends, and nourishing my body in every way, it gets me connected emotionally to what I want.

This is a hugely important distinction. Because, deep down, we are not driven to achieve certain things in life just to acquire more paper money, more responsibilities, and more stress.

So, it's not really the house, the car, the new toys, money, or six-pack abs we actually want. Rather, we're driven to accumulate things because of the feelings we believe we'll have, when we attain those things. It's the *feelings* we'll have when we have the financial abundance to provide for our families.

I want to remain fit and healthy because I love how it offers me the physical freedom to do what I want, when I want. If I want to climb a mountain, I can. If I want to bike fifty miles tomorrow, I can.

Financial freedom is very similar. If I want to leave and go travel the world tomorrow, I can. It's not money I want. I want the freedom, education, and memories that are the result of investing and utilizing money. That is what excites me.

When I look at all the moving pieces that make up the perfect day for me, the next step is to list them out, so I can be clear about what I need to create, to bring it all together:

- Married
- Kids
- World's most comfortable bed
- Workout facilities in the house or nearby
- Amazing waterfall/steam shower in the master bath
- Fresh-pressed green juice or healthy smoothie
- Equal partnership with my wife in raising a family

- Beautiful home office with incredible views of open fields and mountains (an inspiring space to work from)
- Clarity of the work I'm doing and contribution to the world
- Having a powerful team to support me staying in my lane, allowing me to do only the things that bring me joy and are my gifts
- Time freedom to spend in the afternoon connecting with my wife and kids, as we play and goof around outside in the mountains
- Healthy family dinner, all sitting down around the table, no electronics present
- Bath and bedtime, stories, tickle fights, providing a safe place for everyone to talk about their day
- A beautiful outdoor fire pit, cozy blankets, amazing relationships with friends, some good wine, laughs, deep conversation
- Time for emotional and physical intimacy with my wife, when we can talk and connect, making sure our love tanks are full

Once I have identified what my perfect day looks like, the next step is to get very clear about *why* experiencing this is so important. Because your why will keep you on course versus being adrift in your life.

So now, it's your turn. Open up your Code of Kings document. I want you to imagine for a moment it's many centuries ago. You're about to set sail on an epic Atlantic-crossing adventure. Whether you're a pro or novice sailor, what do you think you would need to complete your journey successfully?

- ✓ A map of the Americas
- ✓ A ship
- ✓ A sail
- ✓ Wind
- ✓ A rudder
- ✓ A navigator & map of the stars
- ✓ Food and water
- ✓ Crew

You'd probably need a lot more than just those items. However, for the sake of this analogy, let's just go with it.

A Map: The first thing you'd want to decide is where exactly are you headed? In the work I've done with clients, there's been a common theme. They have had a general sense—but not a specific one—for the direction they were headed in.

That's why a map is so important. When Leif Erikson led the first European expedition to North America, 500 years before Christopher Columbus was even born, he had no idea where he was headed. There were no maps. He was just headed west. That's called having some major balls.

For your case, though, you want to minimize risk by having a greater sense as to specifically where you're aiming. You've got to find a point on the map and decide that's where you're headed. Otherwise, if you're just intent on setting out to find metaphorical "land"? Well, then you may end up in Maine, the Caribbean, or South America. The clearer you are about where you're headed, the more clear you can be in doing what it takes to get there.

A Ship: Once you know clearly where you're aiming, the next thing you need is an ocean-going vessel that will get you to the point on the map you've chosen. In real life, your so-called "ship" or "vessel" is your body.

If you're constantly focused on your physical health breaking down, you cannot focus on where you're headed. If your ship is full of holes and you're always working to plug those holes, it's going to slow you down immensely—or even sink you.

You've got to have your ship in the greatest physical shape you can get, so it's efficient, strong, dependable, and capable of going where you tell it to go.

A Sail: Even if you have a vessel and a clear waypoint, a ship is no use without a sail. You could have an amazing ship with all the potential in the world, but if you don't have a sail or the sail is too small, your vessel will never have the capacity to be propelled toward your dreams of new land.

In this metaphor, the sail represents your vision. Without a big enough vision, you'll never tap into your full potential for how far you can go. The bigger the vision, the faster and farther you will go!

Wind: The biggest sail in the world is useless on a windless day. The sail requires the wind and the wind requires the sail for the ship to move. A life vision will take you nowhere unless you have reasons for why you want to achieve your vision. The wind is the purpose of your vision. They work in tandem. The wind (your purpose) is what acts as the propulsion into your sail that moves your ship and your actions.

Still, a sail with wind and no rudder will take a ship wherever it decides to blow.

A Rudder: A rudder takes the propulsion of the ship and points it in the direction you want to go. This is why it's so important you first know where you're going and have a vision of what you want to experience when you get there, plus reasons for why you want to get there, and the control to direct your behaviors so they're in alignment.

So, you set sail. You have an idea of where you're headed, you have a ship, a sail, the wind, and a rudder. However, what happens as soon as you lose sight of the land behind you?

It's uncharted territory. And without any land features, you could easily get lost in the big ocean. This is why it's so important you bring along with you someone who can interpret the stars—so you can navigate even when you're in the dark.

A Navigator: Without land, navigation by the stars becomes life and death. You could easily lose your way without someone to advise you. This is precisely why a mentor, a coach, a mastermind, or an advisor could be one person or a lot of people. They are there to help you find your way, even in the darkest of times.

Food, Water and Rest: Out on the open ocean, Mother Nature can be ruthless. You'd only make it a couple days without clean drinking water and food. What this symbolizes is you'll need time to slow down and refuel.

You cannot become a workaholic in life and expect to be happy. You must learn to enjoy the journey. And if you're starving for those things in life that keep you sane and happy, you won't go very far before you go mad. This goes back to the need for regular maintenance on your ship. If you're not filling yourself up with ample nutrition, you'll never be able to make the long trek to your destination.

A Crew: Men often go about the journey of life by themselves. It's as if they're venturing off on the cross-Atlantic adventure solo. Even with the best of all the previous resources, it can all be for naught if you're lonely, depressed, and afraid. There are a *lot* of responsibilities when making such a trek in this metaphorical cross-Atlantic journey, as there are in life.

To think you can do it on your own is awfully optimistic. Having a crew of loyal individuals to help hold you accountable in getting to your destination is paramount. Your journey to achieving your vision and arriving at your destination depends on how solid the crew you acquire.

If you have a crew of men who only think of themselves, who haven't bought into your vision, who aren't trustworthy, the drama they'll provide alone will be enough to distract you from where you're headed and why you're going in the first place. Your circle of friends, advisors, and support play a massive role in your journey and feeling a level of fulfillment.

So, just as you'd need all of these things in your journey to discover new land, you need the same list of items for your journey through life. That is, as long as you're planning on living your best life!

* A Map: *Ultimate Outcome and Goals* (to determine where you want to end)
* A Ship: *World Class Physical Health* (the ability to make the long trek)
* A Sail: *A Compelling Vision for your Future*
* Wind: *A Purpose for your Compelling Vision*
* A Rudder: *Daily, Weekly and Monthly Rituals* (clear action in the correct direction)
* A Navigator and Map of the Stars: *Mentor(s) and/or Coach(es)*
* Food and Water: *Values Built Upon Fulfillment* (what sustains you)
* Crew: *Brotherhood & Accountability* (companionship)

If you are the adventurous type and willing to incur risk for something great, to *be* great, then you will need the items listed above.

CHAPTER 22

Defining Outcomes vs. Goals

"Begin with the end in mind."
—Stephen Covey

THE FIRST STEP is to get clear on what the difference is between an outcome and a goal.

I like to make this differentiation because, for years, I would set goals. And within three months of the New Year, things in my life would have changed enough to where I felt like my goal was not only unattainable, it was also less relevant than it was just three months prior.

So, when I learned the distinctions between outcomes and goals, it was a game-changer for me. Let me explain.

Think about the difference as it relates to sports. If you've ever played a game before, whether you've won or lost, there's always been a definitive outcome. There is an end result.

Now, your goal could have been to win, to score a certain number of points, or to limit your opponent to a certain amount of points or yards or runners on base. Whatever the case, you may or may not have achieved all your goals during the game. Regardless, that didn't prevent there being an outcome at the end.

The Game of Life is no different. Whether you achieve your goals or not, you're still going to achieve an end result or outcome. The way I look at it is, outcomes are broad objectives. I'll give you an example.

For instance, if I'm setting health outcomes for the coming year, I'll write down that I want to significantly improve my health by this time a year from now in the area of my mobility/flexibility, cardio capacity, strength, and body fat.

Now, to achieve those things, I'll set specific and time-sensitive goals. For instance:

- ✓ By December 31, 2022, I will be stretching at least five days a week for a minimum of five minutes per day.
- ✓ By December 31, 2022, I will routinely be seeing a soft-tissue chiropractor once a month, to ensure my muscles are working at 100% capacity.
- ✓ By December 31, 2022, I will be exercising/weight training five days a week and keeping track of my strength gains by maintaining a detailed log on my phone.
- ✓ By December 31, 2022, I will lower my body fat to nine percent or lower, and maintain it.

So, do you see how specific those goals are? Now, of those four goals, let's say I only achieve fifty percent of them. In the past, I would have felt like I had failed, and I would beat myself up. When, in reality, even with two of the four goals achieved, I could accurately say, by December 31, 2021, the outcome is my health is still a lot better than where it was a year ago, when I set those goals.

So, all things considered, I'd still be able to say I had accomplished a lot. And that would allow me to have even more confidence and momentum to take new goals into 2023.

If you'd like guidance on how to set outcomes and create goals, I've created a free "how-to" video you can watch by going here: https://tinyurl.com/outcomesandgoals.

Avoiding Self-Sabotage

Have you ever thought to yourself, "I know what I need to do. I just don't do what I know!"

If you've ever felt like there was an internal war raging within you, between knowing you should be doing something and feeling pulled in the opposite direction from it, I'd like to address this right now.

It's what is often referred to as self-sabotage. It's the result of having opposing needs that are in direct contrast to each other.

For example, let's say you really want to become wealthy—which means long hours working apart from your loved one(s). The major challenge is that you absolutely value the precious time you have with your spouse and kids, and it kills you to have to be away from them, when you feel like you're missing out on quality time.

It's exciting to think about being independently wealthy, because you believe it would mean having all the time in the world with very little stress. And yet, to get there means sacrificing the very thing you value so much: quality time with family.

See the polarizing needs? So, what happens?

You're pulled in two different directions, which results in you not being efficient with your time. The internal conflict manifests as major procrastination. You continue to stress out about how you should be working when you're not with them, but all you do is waste time.

It's a vicious cycle and one that can bring a ton of shame and anger.

So, what's the solution?

You have to get clear on how you prioritize your values.

Values

More often than not, our values have been instilled within us by past experiences of pain or pleasure and by other influences like your parents, family, friends, and society at large.

The challenge with this is, typically, people will do more to avoid pain than they will to gain pleasure. So, if you hate conflict with others, you'll do more to avoid it than you will to maintain an open line of communication—even if you value open communication.

So first, what you must do is find out what your current values are. Because we all have values we are attracted to and values we are repelled by. The trick is to list them out so you can intentionally change them and create greater ease of achieving fulfillment in life.

Often, as men, our past traumas in life have been the way our values were instilled within us. So, for the vast majority of us, we never intentionally chose our values. Rather, our need to protect ourselves from pain is what established them.

The first time I did the process of identifying the values I move toward and those I move away from, it was mind-blowing. I could literally see—on paper—values that were directly in contrast to one another. It triggered memories of events when these contrasts of values played out.

I felt like Neo when he saw the Matrix for the first time. It became clear why I did or did not do the things I set out to do in my life. That is why it is so important that you schedule time to become clear on your values as well, otherwise, again, this book will only serve as a "jacuzzi moment" if you don't do the work.

(If you want to take your life to the next level, I recommend you get plugged in at JohnnyKing.com for resources on how to reconstruct your values for success and fulfillment in greater depth than is achievable in this book.)

I teach a process for how you can become clear with what your values are, both those you're attracted to and those you're repelled by, so you can list them out on paper. From there, you can systematically prioritize them and/or eliminate those that do not serve you.

If you are in a relationship, whether intimate or platonic, with someone who has differing values than you have, there are going to be major challenges. If you work for a company where your values do not align with theirs, there are going to be problems. And if you live your life out of alignment with your most deep-seated values, you are going to feel a *massive* upswell of inner turmoil. Anytime we feel like we are at war within ourselves, it can always be traced back to a conflict in someone's values.

Without a clear picture of what you do and do not value, your life will continue to feel baseless. Our values are what allow us to feel grounded such that, when the storms of adversity come, we don't break, but we're able to adapt and remain centered. Becoming Kings in our lives is about supporting one another toward what we value most, because it's only through doing so that we'll be able to spend more time there, thus enjoying our lives as much as humanly possible.

Now that you know this, whether you seek out my help or someone else's, it is imperative you do the work to align yourself and your values. Otherwise, you will forever live your life in pursuit of a dream that eludes you. Aligning your values is *that* important!

LAST STEPS

Taking a Detox

"There is no WiFi in the forest, but I promise you will find a better connection."

—Anonymous

Standing Guard

IT IS BECOMING MORE and more difficult to determine what is and is not factual information these days.

For instance, at first, I'm a skeptic about anything I see or read on the Internet or social media. If you haven't already seen it, I highly recommend you watch *The Social Dilemma* on Netflix, in reference to this topic. Photo and video editing software have become so advanced, you can see extremely convincing content online, only to find out it's fake.

Because of this, I'm finding myself hesitant even to trust most people—at least until they prove they're trustworthy.

You and I have to be very diligent about what we take into our thoughts, where we spend our time, and what we allow or don't allow to distract us from both the important and non-urgent things in life.

When I was a little guy, my mother taught me a very important lesson, using an analogy that has proven to be increasingly relevant the older I get.

What she asked me was, "Johnny, if you were to have a cup made of glass that was completely covered in dried mud and you wanted to clean it, what would be the most effective way to do it, if you weren't able to use any water? Would you take your fingernail and scrape away at the mud? Would you use a spoon or knife? A rag? How long would it take till you had it completely clean?"

I shrugged my shoulders, saying I thought it would take a *long* time to clean it if I didn't have any water.

"Exactly!" she exclaimed. "You could spend hours working to clean that glass, if you weren't able to add anything pure to it. But if you *did* have water, you could spend no physical effort to clean that dirty glass, just by setting it under the faucet and letting pure water continually run into it. Over time, all of that mud will eventually be washed away." The cool part about this analogy is that your thoughts work exactly the same way!

She went on to teach me, "If you pour mud or dirt into your mind then all that will come out of you is more dirt. The world already threatens you with more dirt and mud than one person can consume. It's overwhelming. You must be committed to pouring as much clean, positive content into your thoughts, to clean out all the crap life throws at you. Without being intentional about what you pour into your mind, your experience will forever be murky."

Because of this idea, I've created a daily practice where I keep score of how I'm counteracting the shit that inevitably gets consumed by my being on social media, crossing paths with negative people, etc.

The way I see it is—as we've already established—it's awfully difficult to manage something you do not measure. That's why tracking your time, tracking your food intake, and tracking all the good going on in your life is so vitally important.

If you're not intentionally setting this as a daily practice, your thoughts and your life will be consumed by the shit-producing monster that wants to pour crap into your head each and every waking moment of the day.

That is why my mother used to say, "Johnny, you must stand guard at the door of your thoughts. You must defend what you allow and don't allow into your mind."

And I'm passing along the same wisdom to you, brother. There is nothing more important than your willingness to protect yourself from the garbage that wants to be ingested.

The quality of your life is directly proportional to how much garbage you allow to infiltrate your body, mind, and relationships. If you allow toxic food and substances into your body, there will be an effect. If you allow toxic information, salacious headlines, and gossip into your thoughts, there will be an effect. And if you allow toxic people into your life, there will be a lasting effect.

If this has already happened, though, there are ways to cleanse yourself.

Take a Life Detox

I believe one of the hardest things to do in life is NOT ONLY to raise your standards, but to KEEP them raised. Taking a hard, honest look at your results based on how you spend your time, who you spend it with, and the decisions you make throughout your day is a real challenge.

If you're unhappy with what you're producing, then it could be because of what you're taking in. In that case, I highly recommend taking a mental, physical, and relational detox.

It's time you sit down and audit the information, food, substances, and people you have been allowing in your life that are toxic.

If you're curious on where to start, here's what I do to stand guard at the door of my own happiness. I'll tell you now, though: it's rigorous and always evolving.

While most people eat crap food, drink toxic beverages, indulge in activities that waste hours upon hours each week, and surround themselves with those who do not lift them up or hold them to their highest potential, I aim to keep things as efficient and positive as possible.

I allow very few unhealthy foods, if any, into my house. So, even when I do get those occasional cravings, I have nothing bad to reach for.

I don't read any news articles or allow notifications to pop up on any of my devices. My belief is that my greatest assets are my time and where I put my energy and focus. I have enough people in my life who can keep me well-informed, if the sky is falling.

I've been on this planet long enough to have experienced major market corrections, bird flus, swine flus, Y2K, gold and silver booms, 9/11, divorce, loss of loved ones, global pandemics, and shortages in toilet paper, among many other major threats to the well-being of my everyday life.

And guess what? Although many of those things have been tragic, I've not allowed a single one of them to control my own personal power by stressing out, sticking my head in the sand, or giving my power away over them.

I've even let go of nurturing close friendships with anyone who wasn't raising me up and weren't equally interested in being lifted, as well.

The most important thing is for you to look at what influences you and your thoughts.

Healthy Boundaries

What are some boundaries you need to impose in your life?

For me, I've set up restrictions on my phone and other devices, to limit my time spent on social media. I've deleted all streaming video apps from my devices other than on my TVs. I do not have any games on any of my devices.

Like I mentioned, I do not allow bad food into my house. If I want ice cream, I'll go get one serving of it. If I want unhealthy carbs, I go out to a restaurant to get them. I do not watch the news.

When I'm driving, I split time between listening to music and listening to audio books, podcasts, etc. Or I spend that time calling people back who have left me messages.

I have cut out any friendships that aren't challenging me to be the best version of myself, and I'm blessed to have so many amazing friends across the world. And yet, with limited time, I can allow only a select few people into my innermost circle.

Do you have friends and mentors who are there to support you in determining the quality of life you want to have? If not, then you must be more rigorous about surrounding yourself with those who represent and support your vision. I'm constantly weeding out people who refuse to grow and live positively.

This is a difficult process to undertake at times. However, you've got to ask yourself, "What value are they bringing to my life? Are they receptive to the value I'm bringing to theirs?"

Are they in your life just for adventure and hanging out socially? Are they there because they're funny? Are they in your life because they support your spiritual health? Is your friend someone who holds you to a higher standard, when it comes to your physical health? Are they positive, or are they always complaining? Is there mutual interest in each other, or is it always about them and their problems? Are you friends with them only because it makes you feel good about yourself, when you're able to lift them up?

I've said this before, however it bears repeating. The truth is your life, your physical health, the amount of money you make, and the standard you have for your plutonic and/or intimate relationships with friends or your partner are all based upon what you're willing to tolerate and accept in life.

I absolutely loved what Sanyika "the Firestarter" Street had to say about raising *his* standards, when he appeared on my podcast. He said, "I no longer play the game of good versus bad. I no longer play the game of right versus wrong.

"However, *now*, I *do* play the game of effective or ineffective. I ask myself, is [this action] effectively leading me toward my desired outcome? ... Because, if you don't want to be the victim, the villain, or the savior [in your life], who do you *really* want to be?

"For me, I want to become *sovereign*—Congruent. Self-regulating. A man with the ability to govern himself and his [emotional] state."

That's precisely it. To raise your standards is to declare you are no longer willing to play the game the way most people play it. Rather, you choose to level up and focus on being the King of your Kingdoms.

In my pursuit of always becoming better, I created a support network, tools, and processes to hold me accountable.

Progress Scorecard

A tool I've come to love is my daily/weekly Progress Scorecard.

As we've discussed, I've learned over the years it's extremely difficult to manage progress in any area of life if you're not willing to measure it.

For instance, how difficult would it be to determine a winner in sports, if we didn't keep score?

The only difference in your life is you're not in competition with anyone other than yourself. Meaning, you get to choose who you want to be. There are two versions of you who can play this game of life. I've previously referred to them as the

Ordinary Man, and the Extraordinary Man. You know, Robert the Bruce and King Leonidas.

You can choose to be the version that plays it safe. The one who thinks small, believes in the lies you tell yourself, that you're not smart enough and not good enough to do the things you've always dreamed of. Or, you can be the version that steps up and doesn't accept mediocrity. The version that overcomes limiting beliefs, the version that focuses on purpose and creates a life of abundance and fulfillment.

Truth be told, in every moment, you have the choice of which version you're willing to accept. I choose to believe you wouldn't be reading this book if you were okay with settling in life.

The day-to-day decisions don't need to be difficult. The key is to systematically replace bad habits with healthier ones. Those that move you toward becoming your best version.

If you've been practicing some horrible habits you'd like to eliminate, stopping them cold turkey without replacing them with healthier habits means the chance of you picking them back up is extremely high.

With my daily/weekly progress scorecard, you fill in what habit you want to implement, your goal for how many days you want to accomplish it, and, at the end of the week, you reconcile how you did.

It's a simple process. And yet, an extremely powerful one, when followed.

If that sounds like something you'd like to incorporate, my scorecard template, go to JohnnyKing.com and peruse through my "Win the Day" programs!

The whole premise of my work is to support you in becoming a version of you that you're proud of. Through the journey of supporting thousands of people with this process, I have discovered it's neither sexy, nor complicated. Rather, it's straightforward and just requires consistency of implementation.

The best intentions in the world do not amount to much, if not followed up with consistent action. That's what will differentiate you from playing life small. By taking consistent action to become a bigger, fuller version of you, you alone can determine if you achieve the status of having Become a King. Or not.

The choice is yours brother. Choose wisely.

WORK WITH JOHNNY

ARE YOU CURIOUS to learn more about Johnny's approach to healing, finding purpose, and living a fulfilled life? Head over to his website, or follow him on any of his social media accounts. There, you will find his current programs and information about events being offered.

JohnnyKing.com

Instagram: @JohnnyKing

LinkedIn: @JohnLKing

Twitter: @JohnLKing

Facebook.com/JohnnyKingCoaching

THANKS

FIRST AND FOREMOST, I would like to give thanks to God, for it is only through Him that I have the capacity to love.

I would like to especially thank my father, Herb King, for I wouldn't be who I am today without him.

I'd also like to thank my mother, Sally King, who I only wish had lived long enough to acknowledge the fruit of her labor, in my becoming the man I have become.

I'd like to thank each of my siblings, Molly, Katy, James, and Pete, for the countless deep conversations and feedback, that served as my sounding board throughout the years.

I would like to thank Christine Hassler for her intuitive guidance and insight through her coaching, programs, and book, *Expectation Hangover*. My life is forever changed; thanks to your insight and support. The breakthroughs I've experienced through your coaching have been hugely instrumental in writing this book.

And lastly, I'd like to thank all of my amazing friends and brothers, who have challenged and encouraged me through this pursuit of Becoming Kings. This book is for you.

ABOUT THE AUTHOR

BEFORE JOHNNY KING became a men's transformational coach to help them reach their highest potential, he first had to discover his own. Amidst the recession of 2010, Johnny was broke: $35,000 in debt, jobless, and picking up the pieces of a failed marriage. He thought he was done... Little did he know it was just the start of his journey. He resolved never to experience hopelessness like that again.

Over the last decade, Johnny has built multiple successful businesses and now leads a growing men's community, coaches clients worldwide, facilitates adventure retreats and masterminds, produces the *Becoming Kings* podcast, and has authored this book. Having found himself stuck in a perpetual cycle of vacillating between anger and apathy, he systemized a process for creating a life he could fall in love with. He's now teaching others those same processes, so they too can own their day, realize their dreams, and truly become the King or Queen of their kingdom.

Johnny's podcast, *Becoming Kings*, has featured such guests as Lewis Howes (*The School of Greatness* podcast), Ryan Michler (*Order of Man* podcast), and Alison Armstrong (*UnderstandMen.com*). Johnny has facilitated leadership workshops for such companies as USBank, Scottrade, Edward Jones, and Enterprise.

Made in United States
Orlando, FL
06 June 2023